SATs P[ractice] in Science

AGE 11

Rhona Whiteford and Jim Fitzsimmons
Illustrated by Sara Silcock

The National Curriculum for England and Wales requires all 11 year-olds in the final year of Primary school (Key Stage 2) to be tested in English, Mathematics and Science. These tests are called SATs (Standard Assessment Tasks), and are completed during the normal school day. There is a national timetable for the tests. Their purpose is to give schools information about what children are achieving compared to others of the same age, and to highlight areas where help is needed. This book will help you to prepare your child for the SATs in Science. Although the SATs are taken at age 11, this book may be used for practice throughout Year 6.

How to help your child

a Working together
If you work through each test with your child, you may discover areas where extra practice is needed.

b Test conditions
The SATs are timed at this stage, so you can use this book to prepare your child for real test conditions. Encourage them to work independently and with good concentration. The time allowed for each test is shown in the chart on the left, but do not be too strict about timing if your child is anxious. Do one test at a time, starting at the beginning of the book and working as far as you can through the three Test Groups (1, 2 and 3). Read each test together before your child starts to work through it.

Although Science is essentially a practical subject, it does require the collection and analysis of data, and the SATs reflect this aspect of an investigation.

- Keep sessions short and frequent, perhaps one test per day.
- Make sure you and your child are relaxed and have a quiet place in which to work.
- Avoid putting your child under pressure.
- Build your child's confidence by offering plenty of praise and encouragement.

The only home learning programme supported by the NCPTA

Life Processes and Living Things

TEST 1   Living and non-living things

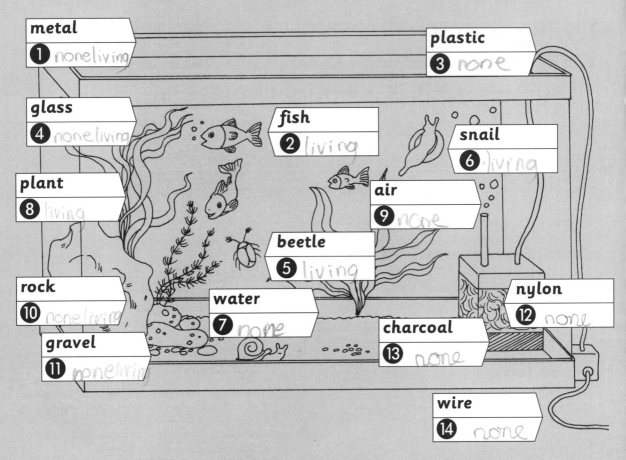

- metal — ① non living
- plastic — ③ none
- glass — ④ non living
- fish — ② living
- snail — ⑥ living
- plant — ⑧ living
- air — ⑨ none
- beetle — ⑤ living
- rock — ⑩ non living
- water — ⑦ none
- nylon — ⑫ none
- gravel — ⑪ non living
- charcoal — ⑬ none
- wire — ⑭ none

A fish tank contains a complete environment.

There are both living and non-living things in and around this fish tank. Write **living** or **non-living** on each label.

Do the living things need the non-living things? If so, give three examples.

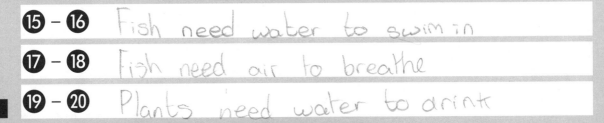

⑮ – ⑯ Fish need water to swim in

⑰ – ⑱ Fish need air to breathe

⑲ – ⑳ Plants need water to drink

LIFE PROCESSES AND LIVING THINGS   TEST 1

A food web

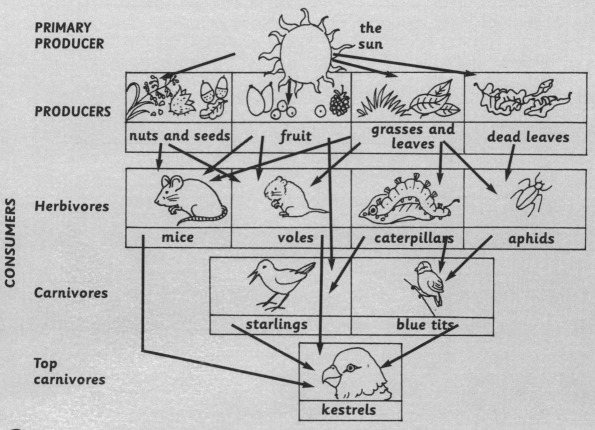

21 Which is the most important food producer in this web?

Grasses and Leaves

22 Which animal is not eaten by any other in this web?

Kestrel

23 – 25 Why are nuts and seeds important to kestrels?

They supply food for the mice and voles which are food for it

26 – 28 What do you think would happen if the producers were poisoned by chemicals?

The plant would die then the herbivores would die then the Carnivores would die then the Top Carnivores would die

3

Materials and their Properties

TEST 2   Choosing materials

Choose the most suitable material from the chart below for making each part of this roller boot. Write your answers on the labels.

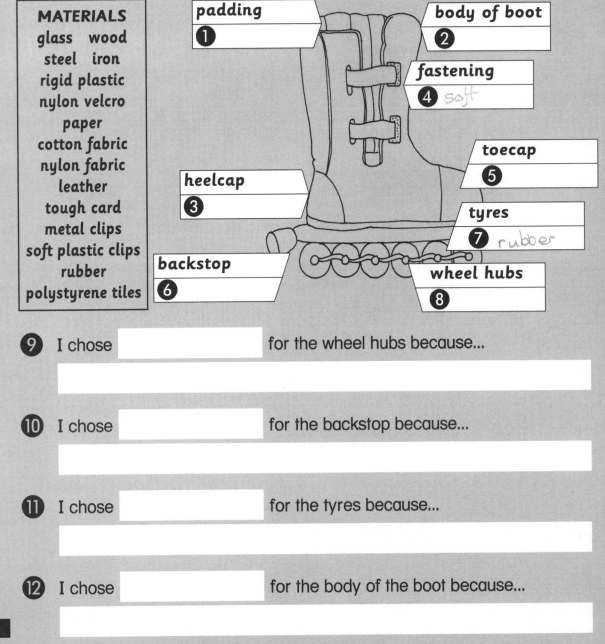

MATERIALS
glass   wood
steel   iron
rigid plastic
nylon velcro
paper
cotton fabric
nylon fabric
leather
tough card
metal clips
soft plastic clips
rubber
polystyrene tiles

1. padding
2. body of boot
3. heelcap
4. fastening — soft
5. toecap
6. backstop
7. tyres — rubber
8. wheel hubs

9. I chose _____ for the wheel hubs because…

10. I chose _____ for the backstop because…

11. I chose _____ for the tyres because…

12. I chose _____ for the body of the boot because…

MATERIALS AND THEIR PROPERTIES   TEST 2

Dissolving and melting

13 – 16 Which of these materials dissolve in cold water? Tick the boxes.

sugar ☐   sand ☐   salt ☐   instant coffee ☐

chocolate ☐   chalk ☐   icing sugar ☐   rubber ☐

What would happen if you put each of these materials in a pan and heated it gently?

17 chocolate
18 sand
19 wax
20 butter
21 ice
22 water

23 – 27 If someone spilled sugar on the new gravel for your fish tank, how would you separate the two materials? Write and draw your answer.

Physical Processes

TEST 3   Floating and sinking

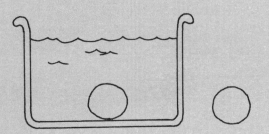

Each of these two Plasticine balls has a mass of 300g. The first ball sank when it was put into the water.

1 – 3 Could the second ball be made to float? If so, how?

4 – 5 Which two forces are acting on a floating object?

Sound

Dave is playing the drum.

6 What happens to the drum when it is hit by the drumstick?

7 How could you prove it?

8 What does sound travel through to reach our ears?

PHYSICAL PROCESSES TEST 3

Electrical circuits

9 Which of these circuits will light the bulb?

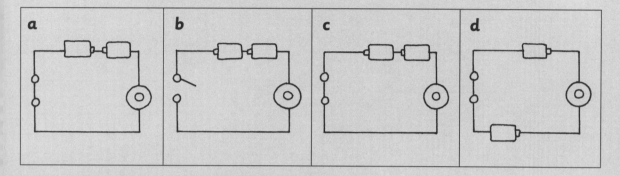

10 – 12 Draw a circuit that will light a bulb. You can use only one battery.

Magnetism

Magnets have opposite poles, north and south. Look at this picture.

13 Will this toy car be pushed along by the child's hand-held magnet?   Yes   No

14 – 15 Why?

Life Processes and Living Things/ Materials and their Properties/ Physical Processes

TEST 4   Light

Draw the light source ☼ in each picture.

These two pictures show a street scene at 8.30 p.m. One picture shows the scene in winter, and the other shows the scene in summer. Which is which?

4   **Picture a** shows the street in ⬜.

5   **Picture b** shows the street in ⬜.

6   What is the reason for the difference?

LIFE PROCESSES/MATERIALS/PHYSICAL PROCESSES   TEST 4

Air

Wind is moving air. Look at this picture. Name three things which are moved by the wind.

7

8

9

a   a screwed-up sheet of paper   b   a flat sheet of paper

     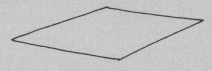

10 If both sheets of paper were dropped from the same height, which sheet of paper would fall more slowly?

11 Why?

12 How could you make the other sheet of paper fall more slowly?

TEST 4   LIFE PROCESSES/MATERIALS/PHYSICAL PROCESSES`

Old and young

parent

baby

toddler

teenager

13 – 15 Complete this diagram to show the life cycle of a human being.

parent

Staying healthy

Here are Ace Baseline and Biff Volley, two top tennis players. They want to be the best, so they must stay fit and healthy. They decide that smoking is bad for them.

16 Give a reason.

17 Just being near someone who is smoking can damage your health. How?

10

LIFE PROCESSES/MATERIALS/PHYSICAL PROCESSES   TEST 4

Insulation

Four boiled eggs were placed in four equal-sized plastic sandwich boxes while they were still hot. Three of the boxes were packed with different materials. The fourth box contained only the egg.

wool   sand   newspaper   no material

After half an hour the eggs were removed to see how hot they were. This chart shows the results.

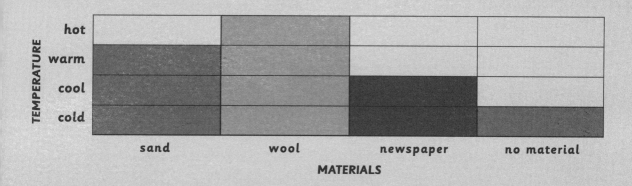

18 Which material kept the egg hottest?

19 Why was the empty box not very good at keeping the egg hot?

20 Why is it best to use layers of material to keep things hot?

Life Processes and Living Things

TEST 5

The human body

Name these organs.

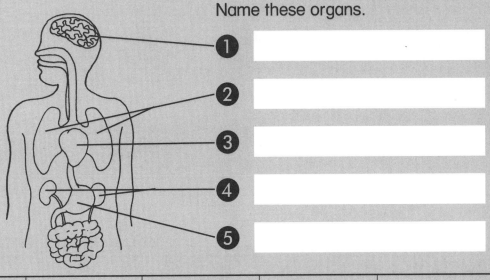

1.
2.
3.
4.
5.

| heart | lungs | stomach | kidneys | brain |

Exercise and rest

Look at these pictures.

sleeping

reading

running

6 – 8 Which activity makes the heart beat the most slowly?

Why?

Which activity makes the heart beat the most quickly?

Why?

LIFE PROCESSES AND LIVING THINGS   TEST 5

Plants

Look at these plants.

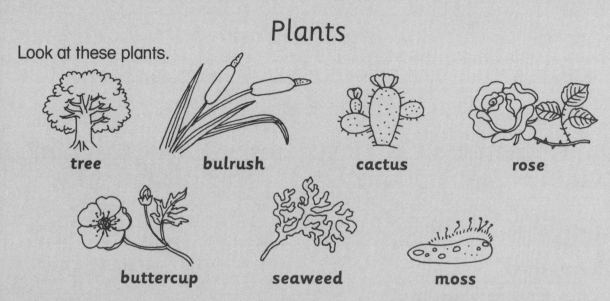

Write the name of each plant underneath the name of the place where it might grow.

in a desert	in a forest	in a garden	under the sea
❾	❿	⓫	⓬

in a meadow	on a wall	in a marsh
⓭	⓮	⓯

Which three things do plants need in order to grow?

⓰ _____   ⓱ _____   ⓲ _____

What would happen to a plant under the following conditions?

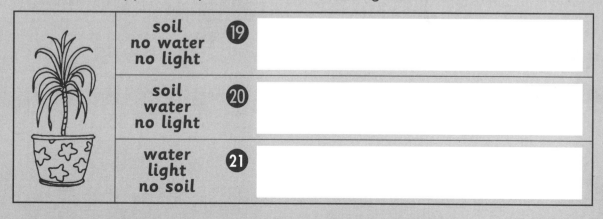

13

Materials and their Properties

TEST 6 Solids, liquids and gases

solid   liquid    gas

❶ – ⓰ Tick the boxes to show the properties of solids, liquids and gases.

Properties	Solid	Liquid	Gas
has a shape of its own			
keeps this shape			
can be poured			
finds its own level			
can be squashed into a smaller space			
floats above ground			
falls to the ground when dropped			
flows through a tube			
can be transparent/translucent or opaque			

A certain substance is ...

... liquid   ... colourless   ... tasteless

...needed daily by plants and animals

⓱ The substance is _____ .

⓲ How can this liquid be made into a solid?

_____

⓳ How can it be made into a gas?

_____

14

MATERIALS AND THEIR PROPERTIES   TEST 6

Testing strength

Some children carried out a test to see which of five supermarket carrier bags was the strongest. They used a spring balance and some large pebbles.

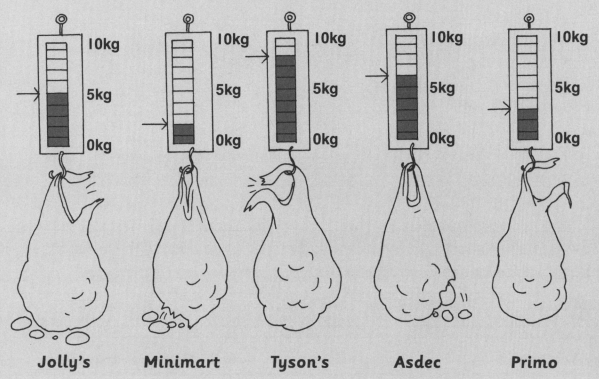

Jolly's   Minimart   Tyson's   Asdec   Primo

The bags broke when the weight of the pebbles was too great for their strength. The top weight each bag could carry is recorded on the balances. The point at which the bag split is also shown.

20 Which bag was the weakest?

21 Which bag was the strongest?

22 In which places did the bags split?

23 Which were the two strongest bags?

24 How could supermarkets improve their bags?

Physical Processes

TEST 7　　　　　　　　Friction

Some children wanted to find out how far a toy car would roll on different surfaces.

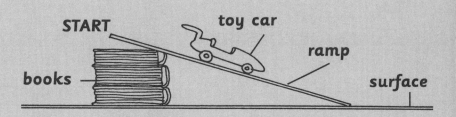

Using the same slope each time, they rolled the car down a ramp on to six different surfaces, to see which surface produced the least friction and so let the car roll the furthest.

The car travelled 25cm on short grass, and 12 cm on soil. Think about the other four surfaces listed in the chart, and then write each of these distances in what you judge to be the correct box.

| ① 5 m | ② 2 cm | ③ 1.5 m | ④ 20 cm |

Surface	Distance travelled
smooth wooden floor	
short grass	25 cm
deep-pile carpet	
smooth PE mat	
rough concrete path	
soil	12 cm

⑤ What is the force that provided resistance and slowed the car down?

⑥ Which surface provided the most friction?

⑦ Which surface provided the least friction?

⑧ What is the force that pulled the car down the slope?

PHYSICAL PROCESSES   TEST 7

9 – 13 On the smooth wooden floor, two similar cars were rolled down the same slope. One weighed 250g, and the other weighed 550g. One travelled 6.25m, and one travelled 3.91m. Which do you think was which, and why?

_____

Space

Look at this picture.

Moon

Earth

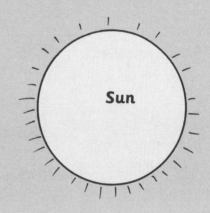

14 Why is a shadow covering the Moon?

_____

15 This situation is called

| an ellipse | | an orbit | | a circuit | |
| a sunspot | | a sunset | | an eclipse | |

16 The Moon orbits the _____ .

17 It takes the _____ 365 days to orbit the Sun.

18 The _____ turns on its axis every 24 hours.

Look at this picture.

19 Is it day or night in the UK?

_____

20 Shade the part of the Earth where it is night.

Life Processes and Living Things/ Materials and their Properties/ Physical Processes

TEST 8   Food for energy

Look at these meals.

a   beans on toast/ an apple

b   a pork steak, salad, baked potatoes/treacle pudding, custard

c   a hot dog, chips, crisps/ chocolate pudding

d   a hamburger/ a bar of chocolate

e   ham salad, pasta/ an apple, a banana

❶ Which meal would give enough energy to a person who does heavy outdoor work?

❷ Which meal is the most unbalanced and contains too much fat?

❸ Which meals contain plenty of vitamins and fibre?

❹ Which meals would be the most healthy lunches for a child?

The human body – what organs do

Write the name of each organ on the label.

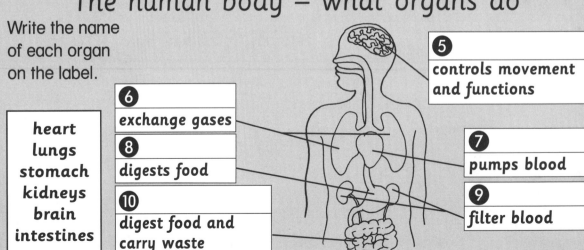

❺ controls movement and functions

❻ exchange gases

❼ pumps blood

❽ digests food

❾ filter blood

❿ digest food and carry waste

heart
lungs
stomach
kidneys
brain
intestines

LIFE PROCESSES/MATERIALS/PHYSICAL PROCESSES   TEST 8

Light

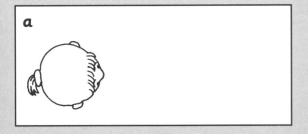

Sue can look at her face in the mirror, but can she look behind her without turning round?

11–12 Draw a mirror on **Picture a** and draw arrows to show the direction of the light rays from Sue's eyes to the mirror and back.

13–14 Draw a mirror on **Picture b** and draw arrows to show the direction of the light rays from Sue's eyes to the mirror and then to the flowers and back.

Complete this sentence to show the path in which light travels.

15–16 Light travels in _____ _____ .

Periscopes are used for looking round corners or over obstacles. Sue is using one to look at this flower.

17 Draw arrows to show the path of light.

How can the torch shine its light on the flowers without pointing at them?

18 Draw arrows to show the path of light.

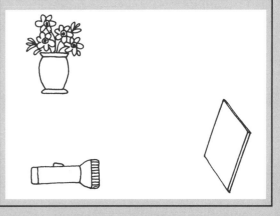

19

TEST 8   LIFE PROCESSES/MATERIALS/PHYSICAL PROCESSES

Seed dispersal

Seeds are spread from plants in several ways: by the wind, by animals or by the explosion of the seed pod.
Here are some seeds.

Write the name of each plant in the correct box.

19 seeds spread by wind

20 seeds spread by animals

21 seeds spread by the explosion of the seed pod

22 Why is it important that the seeds are spread from the parent plant?

23 How are burrs from the burdock plant spread by animals?

LIFE PROCESSES/MATERIALS/PHYSICAL PROCESSES   TEST 8

Separating materials

Four of these words describe ways of separating mixtures of materials. Write them down.

24 _____
25 _____
26 _____
27 _____

slicing   breaking   sieving   chopping   evaporating   filtering   chromatography

Some cooking ingredients have got mixed up.

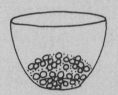

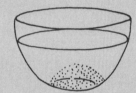

a peas and salt

b ground pepper and water

c salt and water

How would you separate the materials in each mixture?
What equipment would you need?

28 – 29 a _____
         _____

30 – 31 b _____
         _____

32 – 33 c _____
         _____

21

Life Processes and Living Things

TEST 9   Parts of a plant

petal
leaf
stamen
stigma
root
sepal
ovary
stem

Which of these parts ...

9 makes food for the plant?

10 takes in water and food for the plant?

11 makes the seeds which will grow into new plants?

12 makes and stores pollen?

13 attracts the insects which are needed to pollinate the plant?

14 protects the flower when it is a bud?

15 supports the flower and the leaves?

16 is sticky so that the pollen sticks to it?

LIFE PROCESSES AND LIVING THINGS TEST 9

Classifying animals

Animals are divided into two groups:

| Animals with a backbone | Animals without a backbone |

Those with a backbone are further divided into:

| Mammals | Fish | Reptiles | Birds | Amphibians |

Decide which sub-group of animals each of these descriptions fits, and write its name in the box.

- is warm-blooded
- has hair or fur
- breathes air into its lungs
- has teeth
- suckles its young

17

- is warm-blooded
- has feathers
- has two legs
- lays eggs
- has wings
- has no teeth

18

- is cold-blooded
- breathes through its gills
- has scales
- lives in water

19

- is cold-blooded
- has scales
- breathes air into its lungs
- lays eggs

20

- is cold-blooded
- has smooth skin
- has lungs but absorbs air into its skin
- lays eggs

21

Which of these animals is a fish?

22 shark   dolphin

Materials and their Properties

TEST 10   Soil

> Clay is composed of small particles, and water cannot pass through it easily. Soil is composed of larger particles, and water can pass through it fairly easily. Gravel is composed of large particles, and water can pass through it very easily.

A group of children took four funnels. They filled one with clay, one with gravel, one with a mixture of soil and clay, and one with a mixture of soil and gravel. They passed the same amount of water through each funnel, and after five minutes they recorded how much water had passed through.

This bar chart shows their results.

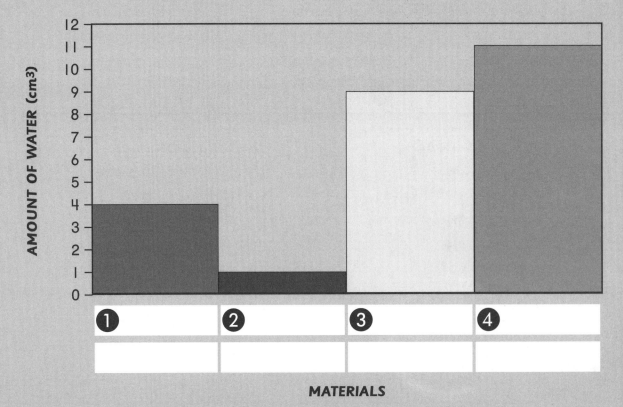

Write the name of each material, or mixture of materials, in the correct place on the chart.

MATERIALS AND THEIR PROPERTIES   TEST 10

Preserving food

Some children had a basket of raspberries. They wanted to find a way of preserving them and preventing them from going mouldy. They thought of four different ways:

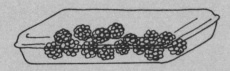

a putting them in a sealed container on a sunny windowsill

b putting them in a plastic container in the refrigerator

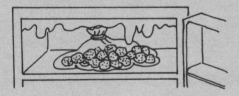

c putting them in a plastic bag in the freezer

d boiling them and sealing them in an airtight jar

5 Which do you think was the worst way of trying to keep the raspberries fresh?

6 Why?

Which two ways would have preserved the fruit for the longest time?

7   **8**

9 Why do frozen foods stay fresh?

10 Why do dried foods stay fresh?

11 Name another way of preserving food.

Physical Processes

TEST 11 Electrical circuits

Don made a simple electrical circuit using one bulb and one battery. He put different materials in the gap (①, ②) to try to complete the circuit.

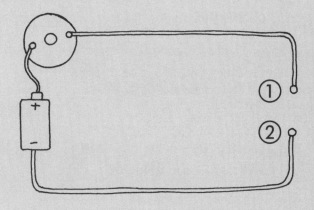

①–③ Which materials would conduct electricity and allow the bulb to light? Tick the boxes.

Material	Conductor	Non-conductor	Material	Conductor	Non-conductor
glass			fabric		
iron nail			tin foil		
steel knife			plastic comb		
wood			cardboard		

④ What is the special name for a material that does not allow electricity to pass through it?

An electromagnet

⑤–⑩ Draw an electromagnetic circuit. Use these materials.

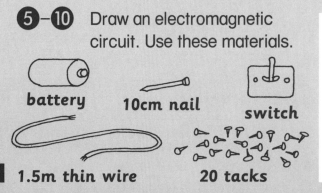

battery 10cm nail switch 1.5m thin wire 20 tacks

PHYSICAL PROCESSES — TEST 11

Electricity and safety

Look at this picture.

Three things which could endapt life are happening in the picture.
What are they, and why are they so dangerous?

⑪ – ⑫

⑬ – ⑭

⑮ – ⑯

Insulators

A screwdriver used for electrical work needs a new handle.
Which of these materials would be unsuitable, and why?

⑰ – ⑱

wood
plastic
rubber
steel

27

Life Processes and Living Things/ Materials and their Properties/ Physical Processes

TEST 12   Changing materials

Some materials can be changed if they are:

- heated
- cooled
- put under pressure

1 – 24 Tick the appropriate boxes for each of these materials.

MATERIALS

PROPERTIES	Cake mix	Ice	Wax	Paper	Plasticine
is changed by heat					
is permanently changed by heat					
can be changed back					
is changed by cooling					
is permanently changed by cooling					
can be changed back					
is changed by pressure					
is permanently changed by pressure					
can be changed back					

On a very cold winter morning, the foil-covered top of a milk bottle may look like this.

25 – 27 Explain what has happened, and why.

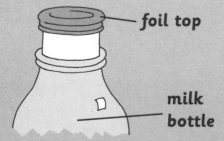

LIFE PROCESSES/MATERIALS/PHYSICAL PROCESSES   TEST 12

Identifying living things

Here is a list of some of the characteristics of a plant and some of the characteristics of an animal.

a	reproduces using seeds or by rooting	f	has teeth and eyes
b	eats using its mouth	g	usually grows in the ground
c	can move from place to place using parts of its body	h	has petals and leaves
d	takes in nourishment through roots and leaves	i	hunts for its food
e	reproduces by mating with another of its own kind	j	attracts insects to help it pollinate

Here are two boxes, one containing a plant and one containing an animal. On each box are letters showing some of the characteristics of the living thing inside.

Match those letters to the statements above to identify what is in each box.

28 – 29   This box contains

30 – 31   This box contains

TEST 12   LIFE PROCESSES/MATERIALS/PHYSICAL PROCESSES

Sound

A submarine has a device that sends out and receives sound waves. How do the sailors in the submarine know when there are rocks ahead?

32 – 36 Draw what you think happens to the sound under water, and write about what happens.

37 The device used on a submarine for underwater listening is called _____.

38 The sound waves travel through _____.

A bat uses a similar location system to register an obstacle when it is flying in the dark.

39 – 42 Draw what happens when a bat uses this system.

43 This system is called _____ _____.

LIFE PROCESSES/MATERIALS/PHYSICAL PROCESSES   TEST 12

Air

This experiment shows how air changes when it is heated.

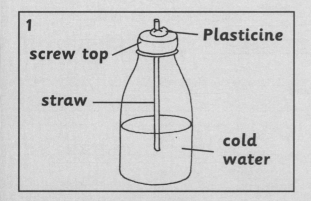

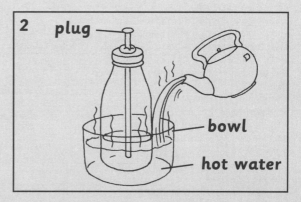

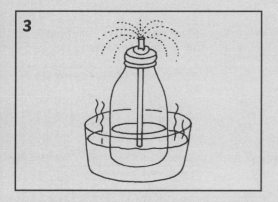

44 – 46 What has happened to make the water do this?

This experiment shows how air changes when it is cooled.

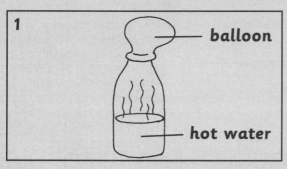

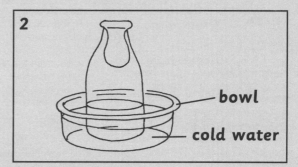

47 – 49 What has happened to make the balloon do this?

31

ANSWERS

TEST 1
1 non-living 2 living
3 non-living 4 non-living
5 living 6 living 7 non-living
8 living 9 non-living
10 non-living 11 non-living
12 non-living 13 non-living
14 non-living
15 – 20 Accept any 3 of the following, or any similar answers:
The plants and animals all need air. The plants give out oxygen into the water. The animals take it in.
The plants and animals all need water.
The plants and animals all need the hard non-living things to give structure to their world.
21 the sun 22 the kestrel
23 – 25 The nuts and seeds feed the mice and voles which the kestrel needs for its food.
26 – 28 The consumers would either starve if the producers died, or be poisoned by eating them.

TEST 2
1 – 12 Award a point for each logical answer.
13 – 16 sugar, salt, instant coffee, icing sugar
17 It would (begin to) melt.
18 It would not change/would get warmer.
19 It would (begin to) melt.
20 It would (begin to) melt.
21 It would (begin to) melt.
22 It would get warmer.
23 – 27 Put the mixture in a jug of warm water, and stir until the sugar has dissolved. Pass the mixture through a fine sieve to collect the gravel, allowing the sugary water to collect in a container below.

TEST 3
1 – 3 Yes, by spreading its weight out into a flat disc or a boat shape.
4 – 5 air pressure and water pressure
6 The drum's skin vibrates.
7 by putting sand, rice or peas on the drum and watching them jump as the skin vibrates
8 air
9 c
10 – 12

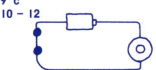

13 Yes
14 – 15 because like poles repel each other

TEST 4
1 ☼ 2 ☼ 3 ☼

	Solid	Liquid	Gas	Remarks
has a shape of its own	✔			
keeps this shape	✔			
can be poured	✔*	✔		*e.g. sand, flour, sugar
finds its own level	✔*	✔		*e.g. sand, flour, sugar
can be squashed into a smaller space	✔*			*e.g. a sponge, fabric
floats above ground			✔	
falls to the ground when dropped	✔	✔		
flows through a tube	✔*	✔	✔	*e.g. sand, flour, sugar
can be transparent/translucent or opaque	✔	✔	✔	

4 winter 5 summer
6 Days are longer in summer.
7 – 9 Accept any 3 of the following: trees, branches, leaves, grass, clouds, smoke, curtain, kite, balloon, washing, flowers, hair
10 b
11 because it has a greater surface area to offer resistance to the air
12 by smoothing it flat
13 – 15

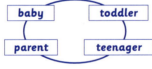

16 Smoking can cause breathlessness, heart disease and lung cancer.
17 You can breathe in their smoke (passive smoking).
18 wool
19 because the heat was able to escape from the egg
20 because the layers trap warm air between them

TEST 5
1 brain 2 lungs 3 heart
4 kidneys 5 stomach
6 – 8 sleeping, because the body is at its most relaxed
running, because the body is using a lot of energy and the heart has to pump more blood round
9 cactus 10 tree 11 rose
12 seaweed 13 buttercup
14 moss 15 bulrush

16 water 17 heat 18 light
19 no growth
20 poor, spindly growth
21 slow, stunted growth

TEST 6
1 – 16

17 water 18 by freezing it into ice
19 by boiling it into steam
20 Minimart 21 Tyson's
22 at the bottom or at the handle
23 Tyson's and Asdec
24 They could make bags whiuch don't break when carrying weights of up to 10 kg.

TEST 7
1 – 4 This is the most likely arrangement:

Surface	Distance travelled
smooth wooden floor	5 m
short grass	25 cm
deep-pile carpet	2 cm
smooth PE mat	1.5 m
rough concrete path	20 cm
soil	12 cm

5 friction 6 deep-pile carpet
7 smooth wooden floor 8 gravity
9 – 13 The heavier car would (probably) travel further, because its greater weight would give it more thrust/impetus.
14 because the Earth is between the Sun and the Moon and is casting a shadow on the Moon
15 an eclipse 16 Earth
17 Earth 18 Earth 19 night
20

Activity Club material

Plagues
and Promises

ACKNOWLEDGEMENTS

Written by Gill Ambrose with Ruth Bond
Illustrated by Wendy Carolan
Cover design by Jane Taylor
Edited by Elizabeth Bruce, Louise Green and Kirsteen Rogers

The ecumenical group responsible for this Activity Club material consists of:
Elizabeth Bruce, National Christian Education Council
Anne Dunkley, Baptist Union of Great Britain
Judy Jarvis, Methodist Church
Rosemary Johnston, United Reformed Church
Steve Pearce, Church of England
Valerie Stephens, Sheffield Christian Education Council

The editors and publishers gratefully acknowledge permission to reproduce the following material, but if any rights have inadvertently been overlooked, the necessary correction will gladly be made in subsequent editions.

Extract on all-age groups from *Growing in Faith*, Lichfield Diocesan Board of Education, 1990. Permission sought.

'Celebration' by Alison Head from *Flowing Streams* published by National Christian Education Council, 1993. Permission sought.

The Ten Commandments from the *Fount Children's Bible* by Andrew Knowles, published by Collins, 1981. Permission sought.

Published by:
National Christian Education Council
1020 Bristol Road
Selly Oak
Birmingham
Great Britain
B29 6LB

British Cataloguing-in-Publication Data:
A catalogue record for this book is available from the British Library.

ISBN 0-7197-0915-6

First published 1998
© 1998 National Christian Education Council

All rights reserved. No part of this publication may be reproduced, stored in a retrieval system, or transmitted in any form or by any means electronic, mechanical, recorded or otherwise, without the prior permission of the publisher.

Designed and typeset by Kirsteen Rogers and Liam Purcell, National Christian Education Council.
Printed and bound by Ebenezer Baylis & Son Ltd, Worcester

•••••••••••••• Plagues and Promises ••••••••••••••

Contents

	Page
Introduction	5
Session One: You and Me	13
Session Two: Friends and Enemies	17
Session Three: Food and Clothes	21
Session Four: Rules and Promises	25
Session Five: Dreams and Visions	28
Session Six: Praise and Prayer	32
Resources Section	35
Administration: Forms etc	35
'Join the Club' - the *Plagues and Promises* song	37
'A Life With A Difference' script	38
Plagues and Promises book photocopy masters	59
Who's Who Book of Tribes photocopy masters	62
Other resources, templates & photocopy masters	66

Plagues and Promises

Introduction

WHY *PLAGUES AND PROMISES*?

In *Plagues and Promises* we follow the extraordinary story of Moses the murderer escaping from the Egyptian court to find that God is calling him to lead his fellow Hebrew people to freedom. From this starting-point, we explore the question of identity, the problem of conflict, and what it means to be part of a community.

Biblical background

Plagues and Promises is based on the story of Moses, found in the books of Exodus and Deuteronomy in the Bible.

The Hebrew people found themselves enslaved in the Egyptian kingdom and longed for freedom and an end to their suffering. Moses, a Hebrew raised in the Egyptian court, was called by God to become the leader of the Hebrew people and organize their escape. As the result of a series of plagues, Pharaoh allowed Moses to lead his people away, only to change his mind and send the Egyptian army in hot pursuit. Once safely out of Egypt the Hebrews had to forge their own sense of community as they struggled to cross the wilderness in search of the Promised Land. However, they discovered that community takes time to develop: it is an on-going and sometimes painful struggle to develop trust and identity, establish rules and formulate goals for the future. We still share these experiences today as our communities change and develop.

Each session in this book relates to a particular aspect of community and also to a part of the Moses story.

- **You and Me** explores the question of identity through the story of Moses, the Hebrew baby who was adopted by the Egyptian king's daughter.

- **Friends and Enemies** examines the impact of conflict and struggle through the story of the Hebrews' escape across the Red Sea.

- **Food and Clothes** looks at some traditions which express the identity of a community. It derives from the stories of food in the wilderness, the Passover, and the priestly garments described in Exodus 28 and 39.

- **Rules and Promises** considers the need for rules. It is based on the story of the giving of the Law at Mount Sinai and looks particularly at the Ten Commandments.

- **Dreams and Visions** focuses on the things that a community holds dearest: its stories, beliefs and rituals. We look at the building of the Tabernacle and the Ark of the Covenant.

- **Praise and Prayer** offers an opportunity to celebrate what has happened during the other five sessions and to hear the end of Moses' story.

USING *PLAGUES AND PROMISES*

Plagues and Promises has been written so as to be suitable for all kinds of groups: children's holiday clubs, church weekends, after-school clubs, all-age weekends away, Lent groups and any other context you care to dream up.

There is material for all ages and it is designed to be adapted. You are not required to do everything: it is for you to decide what is suitable for the group of people with whom you are working and select accordingly. More material is provided for each session than could possibly be used, so that you can choose what suits your needs. It is also recognized that some groups will be large and some will be small. The built-in flexibility means that *Plagues and Promises* can be used equally well by groups of any size: you do not need huge numbers.

Underlying principles

Plagues and Promises is based on the following principles:

- We need communities. Companionship enriches human life as well as helping us to survive.

- Communities need ordering. Without rules a community can quickly descend into chaos.

Plagues and Promises

They must however be for the well-being of the whole community and be enforced with justice.

- Communities need vision and a focus beyond narrow self-interest. Commitment to one another is an aspect of religious faith.

The educational assumptions upon which *Plagues and Promises* is based are these:

- Learning starts from the individual's experience.
- Involving the whole person is the most effective way of learning.
- Variety of activity gives people of diverse interests and different learning styles the opportunity to take part.
- A sense of security is a prerequisite for learning.
- Having fun contributes to an experience of God as love.

All ages together

Plagues and Promises lends itself to all-age activity because of its emphasis on community. It provides plenty of opportunities for everyone to contribute quite naturally, whatever their age and experience.

Learning in all-age groups is valuable for everyone. Children and young people come to know and appreciate attitudes and values which adults wish to pass on but find difficult to express in words. Adults can be reminded of Jesus' teaching that we should have child-like qualities such as trust and openness. A child's viewpoint can often challenge adults to reconsider their attitudes.

Today more and more churches are using all-age approaches to worship and learning. Whether you have experience of this or not, here are a few hints to assist in the planning and leading of all-age groups.

'The 'all-age' experience takes place when –

- a group of people of various ages, including both adults and children, meet together for a common purpose.
- it is recognized that everyone has a contribution to make from which others can learn.
- the activity encourages people to reflect on their experience and share it with others so that everybody can learn from it.
- the people leading see their role as helping and encouraging this process rather than teaching.'

(from *Growing in Faith,* Lichfield Diocesan Board of Education, 1990.)

Since there are no experts and everyone is a learner when it comes to the planning of all-age events, the planning and leading are usually best done by a group rather than by an individual. People of all ages should be involved in that group. Bear in mind the need to plan for sessions in which everyone learns and everyone contributes.

Review your planning and consider how the session/day will be for a 5-year-old, for a 9-year-old, for a 50-year-old and so on!

There are many people in our communities who have learning difficulties. There are also many who experience considerable loneliness, especially during holidays when some facilities are closed. An all-age event is an ideal occasion for all sorts of people to join in, so why not make sure there are one or two extra helpers and make an effort to involve everyone?

A purposeful, confident group can be created by planning carefully, paying attention to the well-being of individuals and generating a loving atmosphere within which the group can enjoy the experience.

ORGANIZATION

The Tribes

Plagues and Promises uses small groups (Tribes) as the basis of its organization. They are named after the Tribes of Israel, who claimed their descent from the sons whom Jacob blessed at the end of his life (Genesis 49). They were, of course, the brothers who were jealous of Joseph and sold him into slavery in Egypt. The twelve Tribes that eventually emerged were named after ten of the brothers and Joseph's two sons: Reuben, Simeon, Judah, Zebulun, Issachar, Dan, Gad, Asher, Naphtali, Ephraim, Manasseh and Benjamin.

Your group may not be big enough to need twelve Tribes. Decide on the number of groups which you will need and then allow them to select their own tribal identity based on the biblical descriptions (pages 62-65).

A good size for a working group is between six and ten people. Decide on group sizes according to your own needs and circumstances.

How you constitute the Tribes will also be determined by your needs and circumstances. It may be appropriate for these groups to be all-age: there are many activities within *Plagues and Promises* which are suitable for all-age groups. However, it might be more appropriate in some situations for each Tribe to be for

Plagues and Promises

a particular age-group so that activities can be more narrowly targeted.

Each Tribe should have a co-ordinator (Tribal Elder) who has been involved in the planning of the activity club. In the case of clubs which are entirely for children, this will be the group's adult leader.

The Tribes are intended to be units of support. Being part of a group enables people to experience community life on a very small scale and to reflect on that experience in order to learn more about it. Some of the activities in *Plagues and Promises* also encourage participants to reflect on relations between different communities.

Within the text, participants are referred to as Tribespeople. You may wish to do the same.

Note: It must be stressed that the word Tribe should not be associated with the notion of primitive warring groups.

The Meeting of the Tribes

Some of the *Plagues and Promises* material is designed for use with everyone present in a large group. The episodes of 'A Life with a Difference' should be presented to the whole group. The final period of the session, which includes an opportunity for worship, is also planned for all Tribes together.

PLANNING

In each session, activities appear under the following headings:

GETTING TOGETHER provides activities to be done as the Tribespeople arrive.

WORKING TOGETHER contains core activities for the session. This includes the presentation of Moses' story, 'A Life with a Difference', and a variety of ways to explore the main theme for the session.

PLAYING TOGETHER provides optional extension activities which complement the theme.

GROWING TOGETHER includes activities of a more reflective nature and an opportunity to sing the *Plagues and Promises* song, 'Join the Club'.

WORSHIPPING TOGETHER is designed to be a Meeting of the Tribes to end the session.

You are not expected to use all the material provided for each session. You will need to choose what is appropriate for the group of people you are working with. It might be good for different Tribes to undertake different activities and then take time to share something of what they have discovered during Worshipping Together.

For *Plagues and Promises* to work well you will need to start planning in good time. Start early with outline plans and work in more detail as you go along. Here are some guidelines for planning and preparation.

Choosing a leadership team

- Many hands don't just make light work, they make better work too.
- A new project is a chance to involve some new people.
- As well as leaders and helpers, think of specific tasks that individuals might be invited to do, e.g. acting, cooking, model-building, sewing, public liaison, etc. A list on pages 9-10 gives an outline of the roles which will need to be filled.
- Follow the Home Office *Safe from Harm* guidelines, or check your organization's or denomination's guidelines on the protection of children and the appointment of leaders. If you do not have a copy, contact your organization's or denomination's regional office or national headquarters.
- Your leaders and helpers will be grateful for any training you can arrange. Again, contact the regional or national office of your organization or denomination for information about courses and training events.

This book is full of ideas, a number of which will appeal to your imagination and suit your group. Make sure that all those who will have leadership roles have an opportunity to look through the material before the first planning session so that they come fired with enthusiasm for what they would like to do.

Agenda for Planning Meeting 1

Start planning at least six months before you intend to run *Plagues and Promises*.

- Decide on the context in which you are going to use the material: age-groups to be worked with, dates, times and places.
- Decide what you are seeking to achieve and write it down for future reference.
- Choose a suitable venue. It will need: a large communal space, enough room for the number of people you hope to involve, an area suitable for messy activities, adequate toilet and washing facilities. It also needs to be safe and maintained

Plagues and Promises

- to a standard which is adequate for work where children are present.
- Do you need special facilities such as ramps, and wheelchair access to toilets?
- What is the policy of your organization for selecting and screening those who work with children?
- Think about insurance – does your group's existing policy cover this sort of activity or does it need separate cover?
- Inform the local authority's social services department if children under eight are to be present for more than two hours at a time. You will need to register with social services if you are meeting on more than six days in the year.
- Brainstorm initial plans using the material as a basis. Decide in outline what you want to use.
- Plan a general framework for the sessions, including an outline timetable.
- Decide how many people you will need to run the activity club and identify who else could be asked to become involved.
- Prepare a budget – both income and expenditure. Decide whether or not to charge Tribespeople and what other sources of income you might tap.
- Where and how will you publicize *Plagues and Promises*? Appoint a person to be responsible for this.

Agenda for Planning Meeting 2

- Make a list of leaders and helpers.
- Make sure that you have a qualified First Aider.
- Check your organization's policy for work with children and determine how to deal with any requirements you have not yet addressed.
- Produce registration cards and consent forms by photocopying page 36.
- Are you going to ask people to register in advance?
- Decide how you are going to make up the Tribes. Will they be determined by age, interest or anything else?
- Decide on the activities you are going to undertake in each session (see the session planning sheet on page 35).
- Make a list of all the equipment and materials you will need and allocate responsibility for acquiring them.
- What will you need to buy, borrow or beg? Where can you ask for things?
- How will you approach the final session, **Praise and Prayer**?

Agenda for the detailed planning meetings

Plan each session in detail:

- For each activity within each session, who is doing what, when and where?
- Which activities are being undertaken in Tribes, which in the Meeting of the Tribes? Do you need to create different groups for any specific activities?
- What materials are required and how are they being obtained?
- How will you register attendance each day? Who is responsible for this?
- Have you any Tribespeople with special needs or medical requirements? How will these needs be met?
- Decide how to allocate people to the Tribes.
- Arrange a site meeting for all leaders and helpers about a week before the club begins, to check:
  - that people know which groups they are working with and what they are responsible for;
  - what needs to be done to prepare the building beforehand;
  - where different activities will be held;
  - that all equipment works;
  - that you know where the fire exits are;
  - other safety aspects of the building.

Before each session

- Make sure that all leaders arrive in good time – at least 30 minutes before you are due to begin.
- Go through the plans for the session together and check that there are no questions or misunderstandings and that everyone has the necessary equipment.
- Is there anything out of the ordinary to consider before this session?

Plagues and Promises

Agenda for a follow-up meeting

It is wise to have a follow-up meeting to review the club.
- How did it go?
- What worked well?
- What could be improved on?
- What did the Tribespeople think of it?
- What do you want to tell your organization or church:
  - about the project?
  - about future work?
- Who will report to whom and how?
- Do you want to recommend *Plagues and Promises* to others?
- What would you need to bear in mind if you were to hold a similar event on another occasion?

PERSONNEL

To ensure that you are not plagued by difficulties you will need to involve a good many people. Some people will be directly involved in running the sessions, working with members of the Tribes. Others may be suited to a supporting role, both before and during the sessions. Here are some ideas of the kinds of jobs which will need to be undertaken.

Art and Craft Organizer

It is helpful to have someone who has expertise and experience in art and crafts, to provide both ideas and support for those who are less experienced. This person could also be responsible for identifying other people with a particular gift or interest which they might be willing to offer on a one-off basis to the club. If you intend to take up the option of making Aaron's priestly garments in the **Food and Clothes** session, it would be helpful (but not vital) to have someone who is good at needlework.

For the **Dreams and Visions** session it is particularly important to have available someone who is good at large-scale model-making.

Builders

It will be helpful to have a team of people who can prepare the building, shifting furniture as required, building any props that are needed, etc. This will be particularly important for the **Dreams and Visions** session when people will be needed to build a model of the Ark of the Covenant and to raise the Tabernacle in record time! Builders may also put up tents for each of the Tribes to use as a base unless you decide to make this a Tribe activity.

Caretaker

Although everyone should be responsible for clearing up at the end of sessions, it is generally helpful to appoint someone to co-ordinate this and ensure that it is done. The Caretaker may like to create a list of what is required of everyone so that s/he is not left to do it all.

Cooks

These people will be responsible for refreshments at each session. They will be particularly important both before and during the final session if you plan to have party food. They may also help with cooking activities.

First Aider

You need someone with a current First Aid certificate to take this role, or ensure that someone takes a training course beforehand.

Herald

Find someone who enjoys creating posters and speaking to the press. *Plagues and Promises* will be an interesting local event and the local paper is sure to be interested. Good publicity at the planning stage is important too, in order to attract Tribespeople.

Judge

It is helpful to have one person who has overall responsibility for co-ordinating the running of each session. This person is the time-keeper and is also responsible for sorting out any disagreements which may arise about use of space, for example. The Judge can also be available to act as a substitute leader if anyone has to leave unexpectedly.

Musician

It may be helpful to have someone to take responsibility for music in the sessions, and to teach the song, 'Join the Club', and any other songs you want to sing. The person does not necessarily need to be a key-

Plagues and Promises

board player: they just need to be confident in enabling others to sing and play!

Nomads

These people will welcome Tribespeople and show them around if necessary; help anyone who is struggling; be alongside children during activities; and be there to talk to. Nomads can make all the difference, especially if you are running *Plagues and Promises* for a large group of children. Make sure that you give them a clear role, however, and an identity badge.

Presentation Team

The six presentations which tell the story of Moses are quite demanding. It would be helpful to have a couple of stage managers. Details of the characters are given on page 38. The two main characters are Moses and the Interviewer (who should be played by a woman if possible). There are three other female characters and seven other male characters.

Scribe

Have someone to be responsible for all paperwork. It is helpful to have someone to take minutes at planning meetings. It is particularly important to have help at the first session of the club to collect and file registration sheets if this has not been done in advance. Easy access to a photocopier is a bonus.

Treasurer

Find someone to look after the money before, during and after the event. This will be immensely helpful and relieve those working in the sessions of any worries about how they will look after money which is brought to the club.

Tribal Elders

Each Tribe will need one person who has overall responsibility for it. At a children's club, this will be the group's leader. In an all-age setting, this person may simply be a co-ordinator and source of information. Tribal Elders need to go to the planning meetings beforehand.

Worship Leader

If you are going to use the worship material at each session it is helpful to have someone to take sole responsibility for the smooth running of this part of the programme. They could also have responsibility for the planning and co-ordinating of worship in the final session if you intend to follow that route.

RUNNING EACH SESSION

Aim
Read the aim for the session and decide whether it is appropriate for your group or whether you need to adapt it. Be clear about what you hope to achieve in the session.

Think
Think about the people who make up your group. What are they like? What do they enjoy? What are they able to do?

Select
Select activities which are going to be suitable for your group and which help to achieve the aim you have set.

Plan
Use a copy of the planning sheet supplied on page 35 to timetable the activities you have chosen and then make a list of things you will need to do by way of preparation. Plan in as much detail as possible.

GETTING READY

The venue

It would enhance the nomadic atmosphere to set up camp out of doors. If this is not possible, however, try to set out your meeting place to resemble an Israelite camp in the wilderness. Each Tribe needs a base area and it would be appropriate for these to be in tents. The leaders, too, might like to have a tent. You could call this the Patriarchs' Tent. The tents can either be built as part of the first session, **You and Me**, or you may prefer to build at least the basic structure beforehand. Instructions for building a tent are provided on page 14. During the *Plagues and Promises* sessions a certain amount of time will be spent decorating the tents.

As you will see from the picture, hangings across the entrance to the tents made them more private. These can be simulated by hanging sheets of fabric on clothes horses or airers. Add decorations as you like. There are instructions in the first session to make baskets for storing things tidily in the tents.

Plagues and Promises

Each family's tent would have been erected around a communal area. Eventually the Tabernacle was placed here. If possible, build the tents around the edge of a large room.

The central gathering area can be transformed according to your needs:

- For 'A Life with a Difference', one spot should be made to look like a TV chat show studio with a chair or sofa for the interviewer, a chair for Moses and some chairs for other guests. The audience may sit in rows in a horseshoe shape focusing on the presentation area.

- For worship it can be transformed by adding some flowers and candles, perhaps set on a coloured cloth on the floor to provide a focus. If numbers and space permit, sit in a circle around this worship centre.

PA system

It is worth considering the use of a PA system unless the space you are using is very small. With a PA system, it is easy to call people's attention to quieten a noisy group or to make an unexpected announcement. It also makes it possible for people with quiet voices to take part in readings and drama and still be heard. For 'A Life with a Difference', it would add authenticity to the TV-style format.

Art and craft area

It is a good idea to set aside areas for messy activities such as cookery, painting and modelling. You will need to co-ordinate group-work so that the areas do not become congested.

The *Plagues and Promises* book

It is suggested that each member of a Tribe compiles a *Plagues and Promises* book as you progress through the sessions. The cover and first page are provided on pages 59 and 60 and may be photocopied for everyone.

The book can be bound in any way you choose. Here are some ideas:

- Fold and staple sheets of paper to make up the books beforehand.

- Make loose-leaf books by punching holes in the sides of the sheets and providing treasury tags or plastic clips to hold them together. Freezer bag ties make a cheap substitute for treasury tags. This type of book means that sheets can be added and taken out. If you wish to make it more permanent at the end of the club, the pages can be arranged into a final order and then stapled together.

On the back cover of the book, there are spaces for the six symbol stamps, one for each session of the club. The symbols represent different events in the story of Moses and may be photocopied from page 61. You can either cut the stamps up and sort them into packets so that they can be handed round during the session, or provide a sheet for each person to cut up. You could perforate the stamps using a sewing machine without thread in. Stick the stamps in place using glue sticks.

The *Plagues and Promises* book also contains, on the back page, a copy of the *Plagues and Promises* Blessing which may be used in **Worshipping Together** at the end of each session.

The *Who's Who* booklet

On pages 62-65, you will find the text for this booklet. The pages have been set up to be photocopied back to back and folded to produce an A5 size booklet. You will need one booklet per Tribe for the first session.

Food

If you are meeting for a whole morning or afternoon it is advisable to have a refreshment break about halfway through. The food you offer will depend on the nature of your group but it is a good idea to have some people whose sole task is to come and provide refreshments and clear away afterwards. Don't forget to cater for any special dietary requirements.

Publicity

Publicize your event well. Send out letters with a registration sheet to those who might be interested. Put up posters around your local area.

Plagues and Promises

Send out a press release to local newspapers about a week before the event.

Plagues and Promises will be a visually exciting event. Take photographs during the sessions and send them to the press along with a write-up of the event. You will have worked hard so make the most of this by celebrating publicly and gaining some publicity for the work of your organization or church. Most local papers like publishing pictures of children and will be only too grateful for your write-up as a basis for their text.

'A Life with a Difference'

The biblical story is presented in the form of a TV chat show with Moses as the chief guest. From time to time he is joined by other characters from the story.

Make a special team of people responsible for this. A cast list is given with the text (page 38). Simple costumes and props add interest and realism. Some rehearsal will enable the episodes to run more smoothly.

BACKGROUND INFORMATION

Nomads' tents

Since earliest times, nomadic and semi-nomadic people in the Middle East have lived in tents. The tent came to have symbolic significance for the Jewish people, even after they ceased to be completely nomadic. Paul even refers to the human body as a tent (2 Corinthians 5.1).

The nomads' tents were made of long strips of black cloth woven from goats' hair and then sewn together. The tents were usually rectangular in shape and were held up by poles and ropes which were pegged into the ground. Inside, the tents were lined with reed matting which could be removed during the day to allow the air to circulate but provided extra insulation during the freezing desert nights. The tents were simply furnished with a rug on the floor, a few chests and a low table. Because nomads were always on the move, even wealthy people did not accumulate a lot of furniture.

Quail

Quail are amongst the smallest game birds. They migrate from Africa to Europe across the Sinai peninsula.

Manna

It is not so easy to identify what manna was. One possibility is that it was a substance produced by a little bush called the Hammada. This substance is used to sweeten things today by the Bedouin people when they are travelling in the desert. Another possibility is that it was something made by the plant-louse that lives on tamarisk trees in the south of the Sinai peninsula. The plant-louse produces little balls of sweet white stuff about the size of coriander seeds and tasting like honey.

The Seder

Each year, every Jewish family remembers the way their ancestors escaped from slavery in Egypt. They gather together for a special meal at home. The meal begins with a service around the dining table on which certain foods have been set out. Each food is a symbol of some aspect of the story. A hardboiled egg and fresh herbs (e.g. parsley) symbolize new life and hope. Bitter herbs are a reminder of the bitterness of slavery. Lettuce or chicory reminds them of how good life was before slavery. Charoset represents the mortar used by the slaves. The lamb bone commemorates the sacrifice of lambs, and being saved from the tenth plague. Salt water stands for the tears shed by the slaves. Matzos recall the unleavened bread and the hasty flight from Egypt.

People in the family have particular parts to play in the service. The mother lights the candles, the father usually tells the story, the youngest child asks four special questions, and everyone eats the special food at particular points in the ceremony.

The Ark of the Covenant

Moses was instructed to build an ark or chest in which to keep safe the most precious possessions of the wandering Hebrew tribes: the two stone tablets on which were written their rules, the Ten Commandments; the other laws which were written down on scrolls; a gold pot containing some of the manna; Aaron's staff. The Ark was made of acacia wood and covered with gold. In some versions of the Bible, the measurements are given in cubits: this is the length from a person's elbow to their fingertips, which is approximately 45cm. The Ark measured 2.5 cubits long, 1.5 cubits wide and 1.5 cubits deep.

• • • • • • • • • • • • • **Plagues and Promises** • • • • • • • • • • • • •

1: You and Me

Aim:
● To get to know each other and realize that we are unique and precious.

GETTING TOGETHER

Come in

On arrival everyone will need to hand in their registration card at the Patriarchs' Tent, if these have not been sent in beforehand. (The Scribe should file the cards in alphabetical order in a box or folder.) The tear-off identity card should be made into a badge, e.g. by putting it in a plastic wallet.

Who are you?

Give each participant a *Plagues and Promises* book to work on as the sessions proceed. (Photocopy masters are provided on pages 59 and 60, and instructions for making them are on page 11.) Colour the cover of the book and start filling in the first page. Measure each other's height and help each other to produce a fingerprint. Feel free to add other personal and unique details which seem important to you.

Symbol stamp

Stick the first symbol, the bulrush, in one of the rectangles on the back cover of the *Plagues and Promises* book.

Similarities and differences game

You will need: either a parachute, or one chair per person, arranged in a circle.

Stand around the parachute or sit on the chairs. Ask people to exchange places if, for example, they have brown eyes. Other examples include: curly hair; ability to do handstands; one foot bigger than the other. If you use a parachute, change places by running underneath as it is mushroomed.

When everyone understands what to do, invite members of the group to think of categories to call out. To make it even more complicated, ask them to think of something about themselves which they think will be unique, then call it out and see if there is anyone else who shares that quality.

WORKING TOGETHER

Join the Tribe

Divide people into Tribes and direct each to the area you have allocated to them.

Help the members of each Tribe to get to know each other by playing a game such as the one below.

Rhyming name game

Divide into pairs and introduce yourselves to each other. Then make up rhymes about your names to introduce yourselves to the rest of the group. For example, 'This is Sam and he likes eating jam', 'My friend is Rosie and she's not at all nosy', 'Will you meet Judy who I know's never moody'. Introduce your partner to the rest of the Tribe.

Note: Don't let this go on too long.

Tribal tents

If possible and appropriate, share in the construction of your Tribe's tent. Working together is a good way of getting to know each other.

Use the pictures as a guide. If you are meeting indoors, you will obviously need to improvise a good deal, but here are some ideas to help.

Plagues and Promises

See if you can collect frames from people who go camping with large frame tents or who have caravan awnings. Make sure they label with their name every piece they lend you. A frame tent with one piece missing is not a pleasant holiday experience!!!

Alternatively, make tent-poles from lengths of 2cm diameter dowel. The ridge poles can be made with canes or broom handles. Lash them onto the uprights with thick string or thin rope.

Use small blocks of wood to protect a polished floor which could be marked by the base of the tent-poles.

It may be easier to make your tent against a wall, fence or tree. Make sure it is firmly secured!

Low tents can be made with clothes horses and airers. Again, make sure people mark these items with their names before they lend them to you.

Another possibility, though it will look less authentic, is to make a round tent. Use a patio umbrella in a water-filled base. Form a circle round it using plastic mesh fencing or large-hole chicken-wire. Attach the top of the fencing to the spokes of the umbrella with string. Then cover the whole structure in old sheets.

Blankets make the most authentic tent-covering, but are quite heavy. You will need a strong frame to take this sort of weight. It might therefore be better to use something lighter, e.g. old sheets. This will have the added advantage that the tent will not be so dark inside.

Who are we?

Each Tribe needs to select a name and develop an identity. While part of the group is busy constructing their tent, others can work on the 'Who's Who' booklet (see pages 62-65). This contains the names, descriptions and symbols of all the Tribes. Each Tribe makes a first, second and third choice of which Tribe they would like to be. Delegates from each Tribe then go to a meeting in the middle of the room and negotiate for the names which they have selected, giving reasons for their choice. When negotiations are complete, the delegates return to their Tribes to announce the results. If you do not have twelve groups, some Tribe names will, of course, be left over but negotiations will probably be simpler!

Each person can now write the name of their Tribe on the front of their *Plagues and Promises* book and add their Tribe's symbol to the book and identity badge.

Painting and decorating

You will need: paper of different colours; felt-tipped pens; fabric; scissors; glue.

Read about your Tribe and make a display about it. For example, pick out the most important pieces of information and write them out in a decorative style. Use pieces of fabric and coloured paper to make hangings for your tent.

'A Life with a Difference'

Gather the Tribes together to hear the first episode, which is based on Exodus 1.1 - 2.15.

PLAYING TOGETHER

Baskets

You will need: a sheet of strong card 21cm x 60cm or 2 sheets of A4-sized card laid end to end and taped together; strips of paper or fabric 60cm x 2cm, in contrasting colours; raffia; straw; fleece; wool; coloured polythene; beads; circle of card (diameter approximately 25cm); sticky tape; pencil and ruler; glue; scissors; staples (optional).

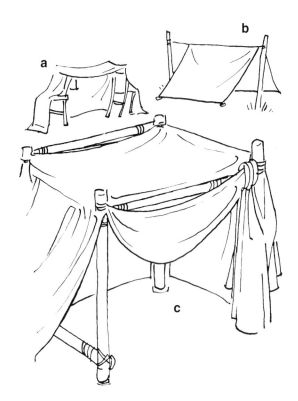

a	Simple tent made from sheets draped over chairs.
b	Even simpler clothes-line tent.
c	Stylish tent made from dowel frame with tablecloth draped over broom handles.

14

Plagues and Promises

Mark up the large sheet of card as shown. Cut along the lines you have drawn.

Weave a variety of materials in and out of the strips on the card.

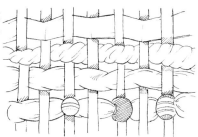

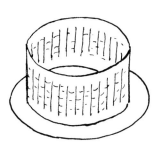

Bend and glue or staple the card to form a cylinder. You may find it helpful to use a paper clip to secure the top edge while the glue dries.

Place the cylinder on the circle of card and draw round it.

Snip in from the edges of the card circle as far as the pencilled circle, to make a series of sections. Carefully bend these upwards.

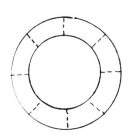

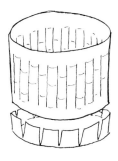

Glue around the bottom 2cm of the inside of the cylinder and then carefully fit the base circle inside, attaching the bent-up sections to the sticky part of the inside wall.

Chocolate baskets

You will need:
3 biscuits of shredded wheat, broken up into little threads
100g cooking chocolate
fondant icing or jelly babies
icing pens
paper cake cases (long cases sometimes used for eclairs are ideal, otherwise use the ordinary round ones)
bowl
wooden spoon
teaspoon
pan of boiling water

Makes approximately 6 baskets.

Break the chocolate into squares and melt it in the bowl over the pan of hot water.

Mix in the shredded wheat until it is covered with chocolate.

Put spoonfuls of the mixture into paper cases.

Use the teaspoon to mould the mixture into the shape of a basket. Be sure to work quickly or the chocolate will set before you have finished.

Put the baskets in a cool place to set.

In the meantime, make little baby shapes out of fondant icing. Draw their faces using icing pens if you wish. Alternatively, use jelly babies.

When the chocolate baskets have set, put a baby in each.

We've been framed

You will need: 2 sheets of strong A4 card; pencils; rulers; scissors; glue; felt-tipped pens; glitter; gummed paper shapes; a photograph or drawing of yourself.

Draw a pencil line down the centre fold of both sheets of card. On one sheet, draw the frames behind which you will mount the photographs (see diagram overleaf.)

Cut out the frames and decorate the borders.

Glue the two sheets of card together, leaving the top edge open.

Insert the photograph or drawing of yourself in one frame. In the other, put a photograph or drawing of your choice.

•••••••••••••• Plagues and Promises ••••••••••••••

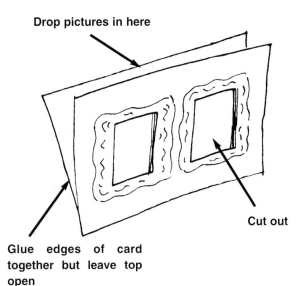

Drop pictures in here

Cut out

Glue edges of card together but leave top open

GROWING TOGETHER

'Join the Club' - the *Plagues and Promises* song

Call a Meeting of the Tribes.

Learn and sing together the chorus and first verse.

Question time

Sit in Tribe circles and talk about these questions and any others which may have arisen.

- Moses' parents were Hebrews but he was brought up by an Egyptian princess. Where do you think he belonged?
- If you had been Moses how might you have felt?
- Do you feel you belong where you live?
- What sorts of things help people to feel that they belong?

WORSHIPPING TOGETHER

Worship centre

In the centre of the gathering area, display a variety of items associated with today's episode of Moses' story: for example, a bunch of bulrushes or reeds, a little basket, some bricks, a length of thick rope. You will also need one candle per Tribe and a lighter or matches.

Call each Tribe in turn to come into the gathering area and sit down.

When everyone has gathered, ask one person from each Tribe to read out the statement about their Tribe, while another lights a candle on the worship centre.

Song:

'You are loved by God' (*Big Blue Planet*)

Reading:

Whoever goes to the Lord for safety,
whoever remains under the protection of the Almighty,
can say to him,
'You are my defender and protector.
You are my God; in you I trust.'
God will put his angels in charge of you
to protect you wherever you go.
They will hold you up with their hands
to keep you from hurting your feet on the stones.
God says, 'I will save those who love me
and will protect those who acknowledge me as Lord.
When they call to me, I will answer them;
when they are in trouble, I will be with them.
I will rescue them and honour them.
I will reward them with long life;
I will save them.'

(*Taken from* Psalm 91)

The Blessing

(*based on Jacob's blessing* Genesis 48.15-16)

> May the God who made us bless us.
> May the God who leads us bless us.
> May the God who guards us bless us.
> May the God who knows us bless us.
> And may we make God's name known always and everywhere. Amen.

Plagues and Promises

2: Friends and Enemies

Aim:
- To discover how difficulties can strengthen relationships.

GETTING TOGETHER

Symbol stamp

Stick the second symbol, the frog, in one of the rectangles on the back cover of the *Plagues and Promises* book.

Struggle puzzles

You will need: a variety of puzzles e.g. ball-bearing puzzles and wire puzzles.

As you try to solve them, talk about what it feels like to struggle with something which turns out in the end to be very simple.

Moses maze

You will need: a copy of page 66 for each person; pens/pencils.

Help Moses to find his way through the maze.

Wordsearch

You will need: a copy of page 67 for each person; pens/pencils.

Find twelve words which are important for making and keeping friendship.

(Note to leaders: The hidden phrase is 'Love your neighbour as yourself, Mark chapter twelve'.)

Get knotted

Stand in circles of 8-12 people, facing inwards and with your arms stretched out in front of you. Grab hold of two hands, making sure that they belong to different people, neither of whom is standing next to you. Without letting go, try to untangle yourselves to form a circle again.

WORKING TOGETHER

The birthday line game

This is a game which explores varieties of non-verbal communication. Use it to help your Tribe learn to co-operate with each other.

Get yourselves into a line in chronological order of your birthdays through the year. You must do this without speaking to each other but you are free to choose whatever other forms of communication you like. Make a birthday chart to decorate the wall of your tent.

Friendship networks

You will need: a circle of paper (approximately 15 cm in diameter) per person; a large sheet of paper per Tribe; felt-tipped pens; glue.

Write your name in the middle of your circle. Round it write the names of up to 10 people who are your friends.

17

Plagues and Promises

Draw your Tribe's symbol in the middle of the large sheet of paper.

Glue the circles onto the large sheet. Look for the same names appearing on different lists and draw lines to link them.

Neighbours

Make one or more gifts for a neighbouring Tribe. Keep them safe for use in Worshipping Together.

Banner-making

You will need: a strong garden cane; a shorter piece of cane; a piece of fabric or sugar paper at least 1m long; felt pens, paints or fabric paints; thin rope or strong string; parcel tape.

Cut the fabric or paper into the shape shown. Decorate it with the name and symbol of your Tribe and anything else you feel is appropriate.

Fold over the top edge to make a channel and glue or sew it in place. Feed the shorter cane through the channel so that the ends stick out.

Attach the string to the ends of the cane so that the banner hangs.

Loop the string over the top of the long garden cane and attach it with parcel tape.

'A Life with a Difference'

Gather the Tribes together to hear the second episode, which is based on Exodus 2.16 - 6.13; 7.14 - 11.10; 12.29-42; 13.17 - 14.14.

PLAYING TOGETHER

Friends and enemies quiz

Organize a quiz. The following questions will start you off. You may wish to base additional questions on recent soap opera storylines and/or current news items.

1. Which captain is the deadly enemy of Peter Pan? (Captain Hook)
2. Who is Christopher Robin's special friend? (Winnie the Pooh)
3. Which nun spent most of her life working with the poor in India? (Mother Theresa)
4. Which Baptist preacher worked to reconcile Blacks and Whites in America? (Martin Luther King)
5. Which 3 friends of Jesus lived in Bethany? (Martha, Mary, Lazarus)
6. Name 3 of Jesus' disciples. (Any 3 of the names listed in Matthew 10.2-4; Mark 3.16-19; Luke 6.14-16)

Bonus question: Name 3 of Jesus' special friends who are not mentioned in the Bible. (Any Christian, dead or alive!)

7. Name 2 countries which share borders with France. (Any 2 of Spain, Switzerland, Italy, Germany, Belgium and Luxembourg.)
8. Name 2 countries which share borders with Germany. (Any 2 of Netherlands, Belgium, Luxembourg, Poland, France, Switzerland, Austria, Czech Republic and Denmark.)
9. Who started off as Jesus' friend and turned into his enemy? (Judas)
10. Who started off as Jesus' enemy and turned into his friend? (Saul/Paul)

Pushme-pullyou

You will need: one sheet of newspaper per person; 2 or 3 balloons; a referee's whistle; 2 goals.

Divide into two teams and give everyone a sheet of rolled-up newspaper.

Pair each team member with someone from the opposite team and stand them back to back with their arms linked.

Plagues and Promises

Using a balloon as the ball, try to score goals for your team, while preventing the person linked to you from doing so.

After 5 minutes, call half-time and change sides.

Note: This game can get a little rough if not carefully supervised. Make sure you establish clear ground rules at the beginning to ensure safety.

Plague collage

You will need: a large sheet of paper; newspapers and magazines; felt-tipped pens; scissors; glue; paints (optional).

According to the dictionary, 'plague' means 'trouble, affliction or scourge'. Use cuttings from newspapers and magazines to make a collage of 'plagues' which affect our modern world. Make a border round the edge of the collage to represent the Egyptian plagues described in Exodus.

Coconut pyramids

You will need:
 100g desiccated coconut
 50g castor sugar
 1 egg, beaten
 a little pink colouring
 small pyramid-shaped moulds or egg cups
 mixing bowl
 wooden spoon
 baking sheet
 wire cooling rack

Makes 6 or 7 pyramids.

Heat the oven to 350F, 180C, gas mark 4.

Grease the baking sheet.

Mix together the coconut and sugar. Gradually add the beaten egg until the mixture is soft. Add a few drops of pink colouring.

Dip the mould/egg cup into cold water and fill with the coconut mixture. Turn the mixture out onto the baking sheet.

Bake in the oven for 20 minutes or until golden brown.

Remove from the baking sheet and cool on a wire rack.

Uncooked version

You will need:
 10 tablespoons full-cream sweetened condensed milk
 225g sifted icing sugar
 175g desiccated coconut
 food colouring
 tray

Makes approximately 12 pyramids.

Mix together all ingredients except 1 tablespoon of icing sugar.

Shape the mixture into pyramids. As the mixture is quite sticky, this will be easier if you dip your fingers in icing sugar as you work.

Dust the tray with icing sugar and place the pyramids on it. Leave overnight to harden.

Jumping frogs

You will need: card; paper; scissors; colouring pens or pencils; strong elastic bands; strong tape or a stapler; one photocopy of the frog template on page 68 for each person.

Colour in the frog and cut it out.

Fold the card in half and glue the frog onto it.

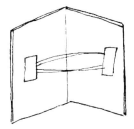

Staple the elastic band to the card as shown.

Make the frog jump by pressing down on the fold of the card.

Plagues and Promises

GROWING TOGETHER

'Join the Club'
Call a Meeting of the Tribes.

Sing the first two verses and the chorus.

Question time
Sit in Tribe circles and talk about these questions and any others which may have arisen.

- Why do you think God chose Moses?
- Have you ever felt that God was asking you to do something?
- Moses did not like what God was asking him to do. If you are asked to do something which you feel is too much for you, what should you do about it?
- Was Moses a hero or a villain?

WORSHIPPING TOGETHER

Worship centre
In the centre of the gathering area, display a variety of items associated with today's episode of Moses' story: for example, a branch draped with red and yellow ribbons to symbolize the burning bush, a pair of sandals, a stout walking stick, a toy frog.

Call each Tribe in turn to come into the gathering area with their banner and sit down. If you did 'Neighbours' (page 18), they should also bring the gifts they made.

Song:

'When Israel was in Egypt's land' (*Junior Praise 1*)

Exchange of Gifts:

A representative from each Tribe should come forward with their gift and present it ceremoniously to their neighbouring Tribe.

Prayer:

If you have made the Plague collage, use it as a focus for prayer; if not, use newspaper cuttings and pictures. Invite people to pray in response to the words and pictures. If it is unlikely that people will do this spontaneously, write out short prayers in advance in the style suggested below, and hand them out.

    We pray for people who are homeless.

Leader: Lord, in your great love

All: Hear our prayer.

The Blessing
May the God who made us bless us.

May the God who leads us bless us.

May the God who guards us bless us.

May the God who knows us bless us.

And may we make God's name known always and everywhere. Amen

Plagues and Promises

3: Food and Clothes

Aim:
- To explore ways in which food and clothes can reflect the identity of a community.

GETTING TOGETHER

Symbol stamp

Stick the third symbol, a quail, in one of the rectangles on the back cover of the *Plagues and Promises* book.

Musical wardrobes

You will need: a large bag, such as a rubbish sack, per group; a variety of items of clothing, such as a hat, a scarf, baggy shorts, a dressing gown, chunky beads; a music cassette and cassette player or equivalent.

Pass the sack round the circle as in Pass the Parcel. When the music stops, the person holding the sack should remove an item from it (without looking!) and use it to dress the person sitting on their left. Continue until the sack is empty.

Festive feasting

You will need: a copy of page 69 for each person; pens/pencils.

Link each food to the most appropriate occasion.

What's my line?

You will need: a selection of items which are worn or used by people in different occupations, e.g.: a chef's hat, policeman's helmet, shepherd's crook, miner's lamp, clerical collar, sailor's oilskins, crossing patrol person's lollipop stick, butcher's apron, stethoscope.

The game leader stands in the middle of the room and puts on or holds up one of the items.

Everyone then has to mime an action which they associate with that item. Use all of the items in turn. You can use items more than once, but those miming should not repeat an action.

Make it more challenging by speeding up the pace, for example.

WORKING TOGETHER

Chocolate game

You will need: a tray or plate; bar of chocolate in its wrapper; knife and fork; hat, scarf and gloves; die and shaker.

Sit in a circle. Put the chocolate, knife and fork on the tray or plate and place them in the centre of the circle, along with the hat, scarf and gloves.

Take it in turns to throw the die. When someone throws a 6, they must put on the hat, scarf and gloves, pick up the knife and fork and start attacking the chocolate. In the meantime, the rest of the group continue throwing the die. The aim is to eat as much chocolate as possible! You must use the knife and fork and eat only one square at a time.

21

Plagues and Promises

Tribal costume

Clothes can be used to reflect group identity. Work together to create a costume for all members of your Tribe.

At the time of Moses, wristbands and armbands were frequently worn, either in battle or for ceremonial purposes. Make wristbands for each member of your Tribe. Each Tribe could have wristbands of a particular colour or style to show their identity.

You will need: plastic drinks bottles; coloured foil; scissors; ribbons; strips of fabric; hole punch (optional).

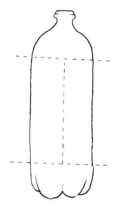

Cut off the tops and bottoms of the drinks bottles.

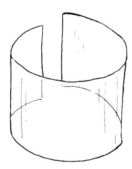

Slit the cylinder up the side and cut it into sections around the circumference to make arm- or wristbands.

Decorate your bands either by sticking on coloured foil or by punching holes in the bands and threading through ribbon or strips of fabric.

Grace cards

You will need: photocopies on thin card of page 70 (enlarged if possible); felt-tipped pens; gummed paper shapes; scissors; glitter glue.

Write a grace to say before or after meals. Copy it onto the three faces of the pyramid, leaving the base blank. Decorate as you wish. Then fold and stick the pyramid together. Take it home and use it.

'A Life with a Difference'

Gather the Tribes together to hear the third episode, which is based on Exodus 12.21-28; 15.22 - 17.7.

PLAYING TOGETHER

Food which tells a story

You will need:
two candles and a box of matches
a glass and a plate for each person
red wine (or red grape juice)
3 matzos (obtainable in boxes in the savoury biscuits section in most supermarkets; wrap them in a napkin)
an egg, hardboiled and then slightly roasted
the bone from a roasted leg of lamb
horseradish (alternatively use ordinary radishes or some horseradish sauce)
a small dish of salt water
some parsley
some lettuce or chicory
charoset (a sweet paste made from apple and dates minced up together. Put 2 chopped apples and a packet of stoned dates into a food processor or blender and mix together until you have a smoothish brown paste).

Appoint someone from the group to take the role of the mother and someone to be the father.

Find out who is the youngest person and give them the job of asking the questions, with help if necessary.

Plagues and Promises

Retell together, very simply, using the words given on pages 71-73, the story of the escape from Egypt. At the relevant points taste the foods which are on the table.

Make your own fountain

You will need: a small bottle with a screw-top lid; cold water coloured with ink or paint; a drinking straw; plasticine; very hot water; a deep bowl or jug.

Half fill the bottle with the coloured water.

Make a hole in the lid just big enough for the straw to go through.

Put the lid on the bottle and screw it on tightly.

Put the straw through the hole and down into the coloured water.

Use the plasticine to seal the hole around the straw.

Stand the bottle in the bowl or jug.

Fill the bowl/jug with very hot water right up to the neck of the bottle.

Stand back and wait! The coloured water in the bottle should travel up the straw and come out in a fountain at the top.

Dress a priest

Chapters 28 and 39 of the book of Exodus provide very detailed instructions for making the special clothes to be worn by Moses' brother Aaron and his family who were appointed to be priests. Use the instructions on page 74 to dress a member of your group. If you prefer, you could dress an action man doll.

Alternatively, photocopy page 75 onto card and make your own Aaron doll.

Egyptian portraits

Display portraits of your group dressed as ancient Egyptians.

You will need: photocopies of page 68; stiff card; glue; passport-sized photos of everyone; grey plasticine.

Mount the photocopied template on stiff card. Cut out your face from the photograph and stick it to the template, or draw a portrait of yourself on the template.

Mount it as a sculpture by sticking the pointed end into a 'block of granite' - a piece of grey plasticine.

Honey and banana whip

You will need:
4 ripe bananas
0.25 pint (5 fl.oz.) whipping cream
0.5 pint (10 fl.oz.) natural yogurt
2 tablespoons clear honey
1 dessertspoon lemon juice
flaked almonds, toasted

Whip the cream. Mash the bananas and stir in the yogurt, honey and lemon juice. Fold in the whipped cream and serve with a few flaked almonds sprinkled on top.

Marshmallow dippers

You will need:
175g cooking chocolate
2 tablespoons golden syrup
50g margarine
grated rind of 1 orange
227g packet of marshmallows
cocktail sticks

Melt the chocolate, syrup and margarine in a large bowl over a pan of hot water. Use the cocktail sticks to dip the marshmallows in the mixture.

GROWING TOGETHER

'Join the Club'

Call a Meeting of the Tribes.

Sing the first three verses and the chorus.

Question time

Sit in Tribe circles and talk about these questions and any others which may have arisen.

- Why do you think it was important for Aaron and the other priests to wear different clothes from the rest of the people?
- In what ways do the clothes you wear influence how you feel?
- What foods are special to you and why?
- What part does food play in making an occasion special?

Plagues and Promises

WORSHIPPING TOGETHER

Worship centre

In the centre of the gathering area, display a variety of items associated with today's episode of Moses' story: for example, some clothing, some bread (enough to pass round and share) and a jug of water. You will also need a musical instrument.

Call each Tribe in turn to come into the gathering area, wearing their armbands. If you have dressed someone as Aaron, ask them to lead the procession.

Song:

'Always remember, never forget' (*Big Blue Planet*)

Reading:

I met a stranger yestere'en: (coat)

I put food in the eating place; (bread)

Drink in the drinking place; (water)

Music in the listening place; (musical instrument)

And in the sacred name of the Triune,

He blessed myself and my house,

My cattle and my dear ones;

And the lark sang in his song,

> often, often, often

Comes the Christ in strangers' guise

> often, often, often

Comes the Christ in strangers' guise.

An ancient Celtic rune

Sing verse 1 of 'From hand to hand' (*Big Blue Planet*) several times as you share the bread with each other.

The Blessing

> May the God who made us bless us.
>
> May the God who leads us bless us.
>
> May the God who guards us bless us.
>
> May the God who knows us bless us.
>
> And may we make God's name known always and everywhere. Amen

• • • • • • • • • • • • • **Plagues and Promises** • • • • • • • • • • • • •

4: Rules and Promises

Aim:
- To look at why rules are developed and how they affect a community.

GETTING TOGETHER

Symbol stamp
Stick the fourth symbol, the stone tablets, in one of the rectangles on the back cover of the *Plagues and Promises* book.

What does it mean?
You will need: a variety of signs which are in common use, e.g. road signs, no smoking, hearing loop, escalator.

Individually, in pairs or in groups, identify as many of the signs as you can.

Design a sign
You will need: paper; felt-tipped pens.

Design a set of signs which describe your church and its activities. Display them as appropriate.

Spot the differences
You will need: photocopies of page 76; pens/pencils; crayons or felt-tipped pens (optional).

Compare the two pictures and mark the 10 differences. Make a set of rules for the household which needs them.

WORKING TOGETHER

What if?
Give each Tribe a different situation and ask them to work together to create their own rules for survival:

- you are in a polar station which has been cut off by blizzards for a month;
- you are shipwrecked on a desert island;
- you have abseiled down the wrong cliff into a jungle-filled valley and don't have the right map to show you the way out;
- you are in a cellar underneath a collapsed building and are awaiting rescue;
- you are drifting in the middle of the ocean in a boat without power or sails;
- you are in a space station, due to dock with a return rocket which has been delayed.

Work out 3 rules and 1 promise which will help you to survive until you are rescued.

Changing the rules
Play a simple game which is well-known, such as Snakes and Ladders. The Judge (or another nominated person) should announce changes in the rules as play progresses. For example, go up snakes and down ladders; move backwards instead of forwards; you can only move if you throw an even number.

Plagues and Promises

Talk about what happened in the game and how you all felt when the rules were changed.

Giraffe game

You will need: a sheet of paper per person; pens/pencils.

This is a novel way to draw a giraffe. Only draw what you are told to draw. Begin by drawing the eyes. When everyone has done this, pass your piece of paper on to the person on your left. Now draw the front right leg and pass your drawing on as before.

Continue in this way following the list below. Give your drawing a name and compare your results!

1. Eyes
2. Front right leg
3. Tail
4. Spots
5. Hooves
6. Front left leg
7. Ears
8. Neck
9. Nose
10. Back left leg
11. Mouth
12. Back right leg
13. Stumps
14. Head
15. Body
16. Name

'A Life with a Difference'

Gather the Tribes together to hear the fourth episode, which is based on Exodus 14.15-31; 18.1 - 20.20; 32.1-19.

PLAYING TOGETHER

Commandments quilt

You will need: a large piece of cloth such as an old bed sheet; sheets of A4 paper; felt-tipped pens; glue, staples etc; scissors; scraps of fabric.

Discuss the Ten Commandments and what they mean. You may find it helpful to use the version from the *Fount Children's Bible* (see page 77). Illustrate each of the Ten Commandments on separate sheets of paper. If there are more than 10 people in the group, you can include Mark 12.30-31. Mount the illustrations on the cloth.

If you listen....

Read out the following instructions for making something out of icing. If people follow the rules carefully as they are read out to them, they will finish up with a beautiful rose bud. Be careful not to tell people what they are making! They need to discover that as they go along.

You will need: 500g of roll-out icing, cut into 10 equal pieces; a knife; icing sugar; ten 10cm squares of greaseproof paper.

Take your piece of icing and roll it into a ball.

Roll the ball into a sausage shape.

Cut the sausage shape into 5 equal parts.

Use your thumb and index finger to flatten one portion of icing.

Roll it into a cylinder.

Lay the cylinder on your piece of greaseproof paper.

Take another portion of icing, roll it into a ball and then flatten it into a very thin circle. Lay it in the palm of your hand.

Pick up the cylinder from the greaseproof paper and stand it in the middle of your new circle.

Wrap the circle around it, pinching the base to attach it firmly and leaving the top loose and open.

Repeat the procedure with the next three pieces of icing, using a little icing sugar to keep them dry if necessary.

When it is finished, hold your rosebud in your hand and turn out the outside petals a little as though it is opening. Put it back on the greaseproof paper and leave it on a tray in a clean place to dry.

Icing biscuits

You will need: plain rectangular biscuits; writing icing.

Decorate the biscuits to illustrate different commandments.

A promise tree

You will need: a large sheet of paper per group (a length of wallpaper would be ideal); coloured paper and glue (or gummed paper); scissors; pens and pencils.

Draw a large outline of a tree on the paper; include branches, trunk and roots.

Talk about promises:

- What is a promise?

Plagues and Promises

- Why do we make promises?
- When do we make promises?

On the trunk of the tree diagram, write promises made by members of the group, e.g. to keep a secret, to 'do my best', to 'love and to cherish'.

On the roots, write promises which other people make and which affect us, e.g. parents/carers, godparents, playleaders, teachers.

Draw fruit shapes and cut them out. Write on them some words and phrases about your own experiences of making and keeping promises. Stick the fruit shapes on the tree.

GROWING TOGETHER

'Join the Club'

Call a Meeting of the Tribes.

Sing the first four verses and the chorus.

Question time

Sit in Tribe circles and talk about these questions and any others which may have arisen.

- Why do we make rules?
- What happens when people disagree about rules?
- Is it easy to keep promises?
- How do you feel when somebody breaks a promise?

WORSHIPPING TOGETHER

Worship centre

In the centre of the gathering area, display a variety of items associated with today's theme: for example, a wedding ring, a Brownie cap or sash, a £5 note, a copy of the Highway Code, a Bible open at Exodus 20.

Call each Tribe in turn to come into the gathering area and sit down.

Give everyone a small square of coloured paper. Make sure you have all the colours of the rainbow represented. You will also need a large sheet of blue paper and glue. If you have large numbers of people, provide several large sheets of blue paper.

Song:

'Moses, I know you're the man' (*Hymns and Psalms; Rejoice and Sing*)

Meditation

When Jesus was asked, 'Which commandment is the most important of all?', he replied: "Love the Lord your God with all your heart, with all your soul, with all your mind, and with all your strength." The second most important commandment is this: "Love your neighbour as yourself."' (*Taken from* Mark 12.28-31)

Think about times when you have broken rules.

Tear up your piece of coloured paper into small pieces.

'God loved the world so much that he gave his only Son, so that everyone who believes in him may not die but have eternal life.' (John 3.16)

God is always ready to forgive us when we are sorry and wipe out what we have done wrong.

Stick your pieces of torn-up paper onto the large sheet of blue paper to make a rainbow.

God said: 'Whenever I cover the sky with clouds and the rainbow appears, I will remember my promise to you and to all the animals that a flood will never again destroy all living things. When the rainbow appears in the clouds, I will see it and remember the everlasting covenant between me and all the living things on earth. This is the sign of the promise which I am making to all living beings.' (Genesis 9.14-17)

The Blessing

May the God who made us bless us.

May the God who leads us bless us.

May the God who guards us bless us.

May the God who knows us bless us.

And may we make God's name known always and everywhere. Amen

•••••••••• Plagues and Promises ••••••••••

5: Dreams and Visions

Aim:
● To consider how dreams and visions can draw a community together.

GETTING TOGETHER

Symbol stamp

Stick the fifth symbol, the Ark, in one of the rectangles on the back cover of the *Plagues and Promises* book.

Pile-up

You will need: one chair per person.

Sit on chairs in a circle. The leader calls out a series of instructions such as: 'If you can play a musical instrument, move one place to the left' or 'If you enjoy football, move two places to the right.' People will inevitably find themselves having to sit on others' laps. If someone is sitting on your lap when you have to move, take them with you.

A simpler way of playing this is always to move one space left. In this case, the game ends when someone gets back to their original place.

Fortunately, unfortunately

Sit in a circle. Give the opening line of a story, e.g. 'As I was walking down the road the other day, I saw two pigs.' The person on your left has to make up the next sentence, beginning with the word 'fortunately', e.g. 'Fortunately the farmer was following them with a big stick.' The next person then has to make up a sentence beginning with the word 'unfortunately', e.g. 'Unfortunately, just at that moment two more pigs appeared from the opposite direction.' Continue in this way until your time is up.

Just a minute

You will need: a selection of topics written on cards; a container for the cards; a timer.

Take it in turns to pick a card. Talk for a specified length of time on that subject. This does not need to be a whole minute. Allow challenges for hesitation, repetition, deviation, etc. if this is appropriate for your group.

WORKING TOGETHER

I have a dream...

You will need: one photocopy of page 78 per person, plus one extra; felt-tipped pens, crayons etc.

Fill in the dream bubble, using words and/or drawings. Talk together about your ideas: what are the similarities and differences? Put as many of your ideas as you can onto the extra copy to represent your Tribe's dream for the future.

Move on, Moses

Make up your own board game, based on the story of Moses.

Everyone's gifts

You will need: each group member's Plagues and Promises *book; pens/pencils.*

28

Plagues and Promises

Pass your book to the person on your left. In the book you have received, write what you think are the gifts/good qualities of that person. When you have finished, pass the book on and write in the next one. Continue in this way until you get your own book back. Spend a few minutes quietly reading what other people have written about you.

Note: only positive comments are allowed. Unkind comments are strictly forbidden!

'A Life with a Difference'

Gather the Tribes together to hear the fifth episode which is based on Exodus 32.20-35; Exodus 40; Deuteronomy 32.45-52.

PLAYING TOGETHER

What makes something special?

You will need: a selection of objects such as a candle, some flowers, a certificate, a Bible, a bell, a cross, some bread, a glass of water, a photograph, a sports trophy, some seeds, a pearl necklace, a wedding ring.

Sit around the display. Take turns to choose one item which you think is special and explain why.

- What makes something special?

Build an Ark of the Covenant

You will need: 2 large sturdy cardboard boxes, one very slightly larger than the other; 2 wooden broom handles; a short length of plastic guttering or a strong plastic drinks bottle; parcel tape or gaffa tape; strong PVA adhesive; gold paper and gold spray paint; a small hand saw; a craft knife.

Prepare the smaller box, taping the flaps inside and strengthening the corners with gaffa tape.

Use the second, slightly larger, box to make a lid. Strengthen it in the same way.

Enlarge the cherubim template (page 79) to suit the size of your ark. Cut two shapes from the left-over cardboard from the second box. Use the craft knife to score along the dotted lines, then glue them back to back and bend the card outwards. Glue the cherubim to the lid of the ark.

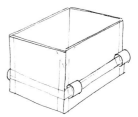

Using the hand saw, cut four rings from the plastic guttering or empty drinks bottles. Attach these to the ark with gaffa tape.

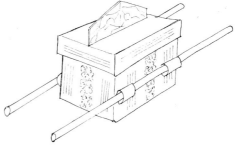

Cover the ark with gold paper or paint it gold, including the carrying rings. Paint the lid or cover it with gold paper, being sure to glue the paper over the base of the cherubim. Paint the cherubim. To decorate the Ark, glue shells, dried pasta etc. to the surface with PVA adhesive, and spray them with gold paint when completely dry.

Make small models of the Ark

As an individual activity, small models of the Ark can be made using shoe boxes and amending the above instructions accordingly.

•••••••••••• Plagues and Promises ••••••••••••

Moses tree

You will need: a large branch; some heavy stones; sand; a large flower pot; coloured card; string or ribbon; raffia; flame-coloured cellophane; stone-coloured plasticine or air-drying clay; felt-tipped pens, scissors, glue, etc.

Put some of the stones in the flower pot. Stand the branch in the pot and use the rest of the stones to prop it up. Pour in the sand until it reaches the top of the pot.

Make symbols to represent different episodes of Moses' life. For example, make a raffia basket; use cellophane to simulate the burning bush; make stone tablets.

Move on, Moses

Try out the games made earlier.

Reminders of God at work

The Hebrew people put into the Ark their most precious and sacred possessions: Aaron's staff, the Ten Commandments, their other laws, a sample of manna. Discuss what you might put in a box like this today.

•••••••••••• GROWING TOGETHER ••••••••••••

'Join the Club'

Call a Meeting of the Tribes and sing the whole song.

Question time

Sit in Tribe circles and talk about these questions and any others which may have arisen.

- God spoke to Moses in different ways and in different circumstances. How does God speak today?
- What encouragements and challenges does the story of Moses present to you?

•••••••••••• WORSHIPPING TOGETHER ••••••••••••

Worship centre

In the centre of the gathering area, display a variety of items associated with today's theme: for example, your Moses tree.

Call each Tribe in turn to come into the gathering area with their *Plagues and Promises* books and their dream bubble. If you have made a model of the Ark, have it carried in at the head of the procession.

Song:

'Father, I place into your hands' (*Junior Praise, Rejoice and Sing*)

Reading:

Revelation 21.1-5

Reading:

Then I saw the earth blazing with sunlight:
I saw children laughing as they learned the secrets of
   the earth
From people who smiled as they shared their knowl-
   edge:
I saw the world celebrating Carnival; black and white,
Protestant and Catholic, Christian and Jew,
All joining hands and dancing through the countryside
   and the city streets:
I saw the city a mass of colour.
Where people left their jobs and houses to join the
   fun:
And then I saw people returning to jobs
Where they felt the fulfilment of creation:
I saw faces full of peace and joy:
I saw children full of food and excitement:
I saw prisons with open doors for people to come out,
And I saw homes with open doors for people to enter
   in:
I saw beauty at every street-corner,
And heard music in every home:
I saw people discussing religion in bus-queues,
And politics in the tube:
I saw babies on the knees of old men,
While their parents danced:
I saw green grass, free from litter,

Plagues and Promises

And trees full of birds.
I heard people singing as they cleaned the pavements:
I saw houses, strong and shining with new paint:
I saw each family with a home of their own
And friends to share it.
I saw people free: to love and be loved, to give and to receive.
I saw peace in people's hearts, joy in people's eyes
And a song on everyone's lips:
I saw dreams being dreamt
And lights shining in the darkness:
I saw water in the desert
And fire in the mountains;
I felt warmth in the winter-time
And heard laughter in the rain;
I saw a ten pound-note in the gutter
That nobody had bothered to pick up.
'Celebration!' by Alison Head, from Flowing Streams *(NCEC, 1993)*

The Blessing

May the God who made us bless us.

May the God who leads us bless us.

May the God who guards us bless us.

May the God who knows us bless us.

And may we make God's name known always and everywhere. Amen

Plagues and Promises

6: Praise and Prayer

Aim:
- To celebrate and draw together the themes of the club.

INTRODUCTION

This final session is different from the others and its form will be determined by the context in which you choose to run it. It contains three main strands:

- a party for the Tribes and all who have been involved in the club;
- a presentation for parents, carers and friends;
- an act of worship.

GATHERING TOGETHER

Symbol stamp

Stick the sixth symbol, the rainbow, in the last rectangle on the back cover of the *Plagues and Promises* book.

Welcome

Appoint Tribespeople to welcome visitors into their tents, showing them what has been done in the club and explaining what is on display.

'Join the Club'

Gather the Tribes and their visitors together to sing 'Join the Club'.

'A Life with a Difference'

Listen to the final episode of 'A Life with a Difference' which is based on Exodus 17.8-16; Exodus 32.15-18; Numbers 11.26-30; Deuteronomy 31.14 - 34.12.

PLAYING TOGETHER

Plague and promise parachute

You will need: a parachute.

This game is based on the conventional cat and mouse parachute game where the cat is on top of the parachute and has to catch the mouse who is crawling around underneath it. Meanwhile everyone else flaps the chute to make it difficult for the cat to spot the mouse underneath. In this version, the person underneath represents the Israelites and the person on top represents the Egyptians.

Let my people go

You will need: a chair; blindfold; paper crown; metal plate or tray with NO stuck on one side and GO on the other.

Pharaoh sits on his throne (the chair), blindfold and wearing his crown. Everyone else sits around in a circle on the floor. Place the plate/tray under the chair. Choose somebody to be Moses. 'He' has to creep up to Pharaoh, turn over the plate and return to 'his' place without being heard. If Pharaoh hears Moses and points in the right direction then Moses has failed and has to return to his place in the circle, allowing someone else to have a turn. If, however, Moses suc-

Plagues and Promises

ceeds in turning over the plate and returning to his place without being heard, then he replaces Pharaoh.

Go for it!
Play the game which has been most popular with the group.

Choose a promise
You will need: a square piece of paper, 20 cm x 20 cm, with the template on page 80 photocopied onto it, per person; pens/pencils.

Fold the paper along the dotted lines as shown in the diagram, then open it out again.

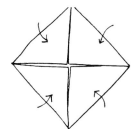

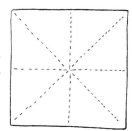 Fold each corner in to the central point where the folds meet.

Turn the paper over, so that the folded-in points are underneath.

Fold each corner into the centre again.

Open up.

Fold this again along the two diagonals and then along the lines which would divide it into four squares.

Open the whole thing out again and hold it so that the face which has four divided triangles folded in is uppermost.

 Pick up the chooser and slide your forefingers and thumbs under the four triangles on its underside. Push the four external corners in and up and the centre point down and you have your chooser.

Now try it out on someone.

EATING TOGETHER

Provide a range of appropriate 'finger food' such as:

- garlic bread;
- chicken drumsticks (or quail if you prefer!);
- hard-boiled eggs (quails' eggs if you prefer!);
- matzos;
- honey sandwiches;
- cucumber sandwiches, or sticks of cucumber;
- fruit e.g. grapes, figs, dates, pomegranates and apples;
- grape juice, sparkling spring water and milk.

WORSHIPPING TOGETHER

You will need: a small piece of plasticine or play dough per person (use as many different colours as possible); a large sheet of paper, on which is drawn the outline of a rainbow. Spread this out in the centre of the gathering area.

A recipe for play dough
You will need:
   1 cup plain flour
   1 cup water
   0.5 cup salt
   1 tablespoon cooking oil
   1-2 tablespoons cream of tartar (optional)
   food colouring

Makes a good fistful.

Mix all ingredients over low heat, stirring continuously with a wooden spoon. The mixture will come together to make a soft dough.

Store in an airtight container.

Note: These amounts may be doubled, but larger quantities do not work so successfully.

You and Me
Song:

'You are loved by God' (*Big Blue Planet*)

Leader: Summarize the story covered in Session 1.

Distribute the plasticine. Make it into a little model of yourself. Hold it in your hands and look at it while this passage is read.

Plagues and Promises

Reading:

Isaiah 44.1-2

Prayer:

Leader: You are God of the past, the present and the future,
always the same and yet always new.

All: Keep us loving and trusting you.

Friends and Enemies

Song:

'When Israel was in Egypt's land' (*Junior Praise; Rejoice and Sing*)

Leader: Summarize the story covered in Session 2.

The Plague Rap by The Strawbricks

Shape your plasticine into an open hand. Hold it in your hands and look at it while this passage is read.

Reading:

Luke 6.32-36

Prayer:

Leader: You are the source of love and mercy,
always the same and yet always new.

All: Keep us loving and trusting you.

Food and Clothes

Song:

'Always remember, never forget' (*Big Blue Planet*)

Leader: Summarize the story covered in Session 3.

Shape your plasticine into a bird. Hold it in your hands and look at it while this passage is read.

Reading:

Matthew 6.31-34.

Prayer:

Leader: You are the one who knows our needs,
always the same and yet always new.

All: Keep us loving and trusting you.

Rules and Promises

Song:

'Moses, I know you're the man' (*Hymns and Psalms; Rejoice and Sing*)

Leader: Summarize the story covered in Session 4.

Shape your plasticine into a lamp. Hold it in your hands and look at it while this passage is read.

Reading:

Psalm 119.105-106.

Prayer:

Leader: You are the one who lights our way
always the same and yet always new.

All: Keep us loving and trusting you.

Dreams and Visions

Song:

'I do not know what lies ahead' (*Junior Praise*)

Leader: Summarize the story covered in Session 5.

Reshape your plasticine into a human figure. Hold it in your hands and look at it while this passage is read.

Reading:

Joshua 1.1-3, 5-9.

Prayer:

Leader: You are our hope and our source of strength
always the same and yet always new.

All: Keep us loving and trusting you.

Bring forward your figure and place it on the rainbow outline, using the colours as a guide.

If space allows, stand in a large circle and hold hands.

Say the Blessing together:

May the God who made us bless us.

May the God who leads us bless us.

May the God who guards us bless us.

May the God who knows us bless us.

And may we make God's name known always and everywhere. Amen

Plagues and Promises

PLAGUES AND PROMISES SESSION PLANNING SHEET

TITLE OF SESSION: **Day and Date:**

Activity	Start	Leader(s)

Materials needed

Preparation

Comments

Resources Section 35

This page may be photocopied for use in your Plagues and Promises sessions. © National Christian Education Council 1998.

Plagues and Promises

Plagues and Promises

Registration Card

Yes please, I would like to come to *Plagues and Promises!*

Name: _____

Address: _____

Telephone: _____

Date of birth: _____

School Year: _____

Plagues and Promises

If you are under 18, please ask a parent or carer to complete this and sign it.

Emergency Contact: _____
Relationship: _____ Tel: _____

Alternative Contact: _____
Relationship: _____ Tel: _____

Please note below any disabilities or medical conditions your child has (eg asthma, special dietary needs, regular medication). Please attach any special instructions to this card with a paper clip.

I have noted the arrangements for *Plagues and Promises* and give permission for my child to take part.

Signed: _____ (Parent/Carer) Date: _____

Plagues and Promises

Identity Badge

This is _____

of the Tribe of _____

Photograph or Self Portrait

Tribe Symbol

Plagues and Promises

Identity badge (back)

Name: _____

Any disability or special medical condition:
_____
_____
_____

---

36 Resources Section

This page may be photocopied for use in your Plagues and Promises sessions. © National Christian Education Council 1998.

Plagues and Promises

Join the Club - The *Plagues and Promises* Song

2. There are problems to solve,
We must all be involved,
We must fight for what's right and what's just.
It will sometimes be tough,
It will often be rough;
But to struggle for right is a must.

3. We sit down to eat,
And we each have a seat;
There's a place for each one of us here.
We dress up, we dress down,
But we don't wear a frown;
And when someone does well, we all cheer.

4. There are things we must know,
There are things we must say,
There are things we must do and must not.
For we care for each one -
All God's daughters and sons -
Whether old, young, or still in a cot.

5. We have songs that we sing,
We have stories to bring,
There are things that are best done together.
So we dream and we hope,
We need vision to cope.
With our dreams, all the storms we will weather.

This page may be photocopied for use in your Plagues and Promises sessions. © National Christian Education Council 1998.

Plagues and Promises

A Life With A Difference

Characters

Interviewer:	May be either male or female. Choose a name if you wish. The character is the chat-show-host-type who has done much research into the life of the guest on their show but who is occasionally surprised by some of the answers given. It might be helpful for the interviewer's personality to shift slightly occasionally, to reflect various stereotypes. He/she could sometimes ask difficult questions and adopt a serious, sceptical view. At other times, a sympathetic stance might be appropriate; when the audience is involved, a sensationalist 'Oprah Winfrey'-type approach might be amusing, depending on your audience.
Moses:	As a character he can either age as required or be the same age with the same costume throughout. A confident manner is a requirement for the actor.
Zipporah:	Reasonably strong and forthright. She and Moses could operate as a comedy husband and wife team on occasion, correcting one another and even arguing.
Miriam:	Vivacious, keen; loves her brother.
Jochabed:	Shy but very proud of her son; cannot believe she is here; is more used to a quiet life.
Aaron:	Confident, not lost for words or nervous, eager.
Jethro:	Venerable old man, a priest. His sometimes high-flown words and phrases reflect the ponderous nature of his character.
Naboth:	A fan of Moses. Would talk and talk, especially of the old days so has to be stopped. A lively soul.
Samuel, Bezalel, Oholiab:	Highly-skilled craftsmen, proud to be involved in such important work.
Joshua:	Quietly confident and strong.
Strawbricks:	Colourful, outgoing types who will engage the audience in the rap. Suggest a minimum of 6 people, but more if possible. Clothes & attitude could be based on a currently popular teen band.
Workers:	Well-primed individuals who know the moves in the construction.

You may photocopy this page for use in your Plagues and Promises sessions. © NCEC 1998.

Plagues and Promises

A Life With A Difference

Costume

Suggest all characters wear a biblical-style outfit but should be distinguished as characters in a play by their dress. Arab-style headdresses alone could be used.

Interviewer to be in contemporary dress, flamboyant and fashionable, possibly glitzy and tasteless like a game-show host.

The setting

A television studio, no stage separating audience from the action, merely floor space. The scene is constant for the six sessions with armchairs or a settee for the guests, and the Interviewer having the same easy chair at all times. A coffee table with vase of flowers, dish of sweets, possibly jug and tumblers.

Microphones (suggest genuine use); hand-held, possibly several when required for audience participation.

Suggest 2 Floor Managers to facilitate the moving of microphones, etc.

The set may be dressed with large flower arrangements or piece of modern sculpture as desired. Flats, plain or painted to own design, may be used to make a box set within the 'studio'.

Script

The Interviewer may use a clipboard with script attached which can be used as a prompt sheet!

Properties

Chairs, footstools, any pieces of furniture appropriate for the setting.

Day 1

Brick(s)

Day 3

Manna (Honey and Banana Whip - see page 23)

Day 4

Commandment Stones (2) - large enough to be seen by audience

Overhead projector (see script note) and commandments written on acetates

Day 5

Simple plan of the Tabernacle

Dry ice may be obtained through The Distillers Company (local) or from a cold store or ice-cream manufacturer.

Smoke machines can be hired from theatrical or disco suppliers in your area.

You may photocopy this page for use in your Plagues and Promises sessions. © NCEC 1998.

•••••••••••••• **Plagues and Promises** ••••••••••••••

A Life With A Difference

Day 1: You and Me

Interviewer:	Hello and welcome to 'A Life with a Difference', the programme that introduces you to the great and famous and gets some serious answers to some serious questions. Today's guest is something special. His is a tale of rags to riches, slaves and royalty, exiles and tyrants, adventure and danger, plagues and promises. So let's meet and greet MOSES!
	Applause as Moses enters. Interviewer and Moses shake hands and Moses responds to the audience.
Interviewer	Moses, welcome, at last. We've been trying to get you onto the programme for weeks now. So glad you finally made it.
Moses:	Good to be here.
Interviewer:	Your ancestor Joseph, the one with the extravagant taste in overcoats, when he came onto the programme he said we'd have a job to get you. You're really quite a shy man underneath, then?
Moses:	Yes, I suppose I am. But when God sets me a task he gives me the strength to say and do what is necessary. Of course, Aaron, my brother, helped me a lot at the beginning of it all.
Interviewer:	And that's exactly what we want to hear about today, how it all began. Am I right in thinking that you were brought up by Pharaoh's daughter in an Egyptian palace?
Moses:	That's right. But I'm not Egyptian. As you told the audience, I am descended from Joseph, who was a Hebrew. He was my uncle, many times removed, and his brother, Levi, was the founder of my family. We settled in Egypt, like all of the brothers. Pharaoh began to get jumpy because he thought we'd be taking over his country; well, there were so many of us!
Interviewer:	But he took advantage of the situation and got some cheap labour out of it, surely?
Moses:	He enslaved us! Put us to work making bricks.
Interviewer:	And I have an example down here (*reaches behind his chair*) of the kind of bricks they made. Must have been dreadful work. And there were no trade unions or complaints commissions for the Hebrews! (*Pause*) Now at this point I should like to bring on two ladies who have played an important part in your life, Moses. Your sister Miriam and your mother

•••••••••••• Plagues and Promises ••••••••••••

A Life With A Difference

Jochabed.

Enter the two women who shake hands with Interviewer and both could kiss Moses!

Interviewer:	Welcome. Now, Jochabed, I should like to take you back to the time your son, Moses, was born. Those were hard times, weren't they?
Jochabed:	Yes. Because Pharaoh was so frightened our people might rebel or cause trouble in some way he made family planning compulsory.
Interviewer:	Family planning of a drastic nature, I understand?
Jochabed:	Yes. All baby boys had to be killed at birth – by the midwives.
Interviewer:	But they did nothing, they let all the babies live, didn't they? So Pharaoh was having disputes with his workforce and with the health service! Miriam, perhaps you would like to come in there and tell us what happened next.
Miriam:	Oh, yes. Well, Pharaoh ordered that baby boys were to be thrown into the River Nile at birth. Drown them, you see.
Interviewer:	So that is what your mother did, isn't it, threw Moses into the River Nile?
Miriam:	Er, yes. But she made a basket of reeds and covered it with bitumen, that's like tar, really, black and sticky, and she put Moses in it. Then she put it into the river. I think she hoped for a miracle. Isn't that so, Mother?
Jochabed:	I think so. And, of course, one did happen. Miriam watched from the river bank, hidden from view to see what might happen.
Interviewer:	And that is when Pharaoh's daughter came along, isn't it?
Miriam:	You're right. One of her handmaidens found the basket amongst the bulrushes and they all fell for Moses, he was such a beautiful baby. But he was crying because he was hungry. I knew that; I knew he was ready for a feed.
Interviewer:	So what happened?
Jochabed:	Miriam came to fetch me. She'd told Pharaoh's daughter that she knew of a woman who would be just right to look after the baby, and to feed him.
Interviewer:	Do you think Pharaoh's daughter realized that this baby was

You may photocopy this page for use in your Plagues and Promises sessions. © NCEC 1998.

Plagues and Promises

A Life With A Difference

	the son of a Hebrew slave? Didn't she worry there'd be a scandal if the press found out a member of the royal family was fraternizing with the underclasses? Moses, did she ever say anything to you?
Moses:	She said nothing but, yes, she knew I wasn't Egyptian. Nevertheless, she cared for me and she gave me the best of everything. But I always knew who my true mother was *(takes Jochabed's hand)* and who really loved me as a mother.
Interviewer:	So, in effect, you had two mothers, two families. Did you not feel confused, or as if you were betraying your roots?
Moses:	To a certain extent, yes. I knew I was born a Hebrew and my immediate family were Hebrews who all worshipped God, yet all the time I was surrounded by Egyptians and their gods; and they worshipped them with as much zeal as my people worshipped God. I was loved and cherished by the Egyptians I had grown up with. They too treated me like a son, as an Egyptian. But I was always aware that while I had all these privileges, the rest of my people were enslaved and brutalized.
Interviewer:	The time was fast approaching, I think, Moses, when you had to decide who you really were!
Moses:	I felt in the end that I had to do something, that I couldn't watch my people suffer.
Interviewer:	And that was when the ah... unfortunate incident occurred, your run-in with the authorities, as it were. Would you mind telling us about what happened, Moses? It seems the stress of living two lives at once finally got to you...
Moses:	I suppose you could say that. I went to see the Israelites working on the pyramids, and I saw one of them being whipped by an Egyptian guard.
Interviewer:	And your response? Did you go and protest to Pharaoh about the injustice?
Moses:	No, I was a young man then, still rash and impetuous. Anyway, as you'll hear later, Pharaoh was not interested in complaints and reason. I went to protect the slave, and I... I killed the guard.
Interviewer:	So your secret was finally out? You chose which side you

You may photocopy this page for use in your Plagues and Promises sessions. © NCEC 1998.

Plagues and Promises

A Life With A Difference

	were on?
Moses:	No, it's not always that easy. I hid his body in the sand and went home.
Interviewer:	Ah, yes. But your cover was blown by an Israelite, I believe?
Moses:	Yes. It's hard when you don't know where you belong. Neither side trusted me. It was a few days later. I stopped a fight between two Hebrews, and one of them asked if I was going to kill him too! And who knows how many people he'd spread the story to?
Interviewer:	So, there was a scandal. *(Turns to audience)* But we'll hear all about that tomorrow. Tune in again and find out how Moses dealt with being rejected by both the peoples who'd brought him up. How he found out where he really belonged. How he coped with life on the run. Goodbye for now!

Day 2: Friends and Enemies

Interviewer:	If you are joining us from last time, you will know that our subject on ' A Life with a Difference' for the entire week is a man in a million. It is Moses, a Hebrew, an Israelite, brought up as an Egyptian. As we heard him tell us yesterday, he decided to fight back against Pharaoh's oppression of the Hebrews. But he couldn't keep his killing of an Egyptian secret for long, and he ended up being hunted by the Egyptians and mistrusted by the Hebrews. How did he cope with living in fear and secrecy? Let's find out from the man himself. Moses.
	Enter Moses. They shake hands and both sit.
Interviewer:	Welcome, once again. So, tell us, where did you hide?
Moses:	I went to the land of Midian, in the district around Mount Sinai. I was taken in by Jethro, a priest, and I ended up marrying one of his daughters.
Interviewer:	So being an exile isn't all bad, then? But let me stop you there as we have a surprise guest! Moses doesn't know this, ladies and gentlemen, but his wife, Zipporah, is here in the studio today!
	Moses looks shocked. Enter Zipporah. General welcome.
Interviewer:	Hello! So, tell us, what did you make of Moses when you first met him?

Plagues and Promises

A Life With A Difference

Zipporah:	Well, I found him impetuous and he did have a temper at times, and quite a heavy hand.
Moses:	I was an angry young man, I know, but I had a lot to be angry about! My people were still enslaved in Egypt.
Zipporah:	Sshhh! As I was about to say, he did mellow over the years. He looked after my father's flock of sheep which meant that he was away for long periods at a time. The life of a shepherd can be lonely and I know Moses had plenty of time to think.
Interviewer:	Moses, what happened out there among all those sheep?
Moses:	Oh, I would think about the injustice being suffered by my people, how unfair and how sad it all was, that it must be changed. But how? And then, of course, God stepped in.
Interviewer:	Perhaps you could explain what you mean.
Moses:	You see, God knew what was happening with my people and he was biding his time before putting his rescue plan into action. He waited for the new Pharaoh to come to the throne. It's just that God's purpose involved me, reluctant as I was.
Interviewer:	Reluctant? That's a bit of a change from the hasty young man who killed a guard in a rage, isn't it?
Moses:	Well, I'm no orator. I couldn't make speeches that people would want to listen to.
Interviewer:	Hold on there, tell us about God.
Moses:	Well, I saw a bush, full of fire and flame but it wasn't burning up. Then a voice, God's voice, told me to take off my sandals as I was on holy ground.
Interviewer:	You're sure you hadn't just been out in the desert on your own for too long?
Moses:	Oh, yes. The flame was definitely a sign of God's power. And all the things God told me about did eventually happen. He told me that I was to bring my people out of Egypt. My brother Aaron would be the spokesperson and, eventually, God told me, 'Your success will prove my purpose.' Which it did.
Interviewer:	*(Turning to wife)* And did Moses discuss this with you, Zipporah?
Zipporah:	Not very much, but he became very determined. He said he knew now he belonged to the God of the Israelites.

You may photocopy this page for use in your Plagues and Promises sessions. © NCEC 1998.

Plagues and Promises

A Life With A Difference

Interviewer: *(Turning to audience)* Now I wonder, has anyone else here today ever had an experience like the burning bush episode? I mean, has anything like that ever changed your life and helped you to decide where you belong? Does anyone have any questions for Moses? Does all this ring bells with you?

Conversational exchange with the audience if applicable. Use the 'roving mike' technique.

Interviewer: Now, to someone else who plays a big part in Moses' story. The man who helped him carry out the plan he was given by God; the man with the words, Moses' big brother, Aaron.

Aaron enters, welcome, handshakes, etc.

Interviewer: The next step in the story is a little incredible, but I think you're going to explain.

Aaron: Yes, indeed. God wanted to set his people free from Egypt and he did, in stages, and he started by trying to get Pharaoh to agree to the Israelites going off into the desert to worship God.

Interviewer: And we'll pause here for a musical interlude. Because we have in the studio today, fresh from their recent tour of the Fertile Crescent, Old Testament chart sensations the Strawbricks! And they're going to perform their latest smash hit, the Plague Rap, which explains what happened next.

Enter the group and perform -

The Plague Rap (page 58).

Exit Strawbricks.

Interviewer: So the Israelites were free, and Moses was a brave rebel leader. Pharaoh sent them packing but, as you might guess, he changed his mind - he realized he would not have enough people to build his pyramids! So Pharaoh and his armies went after the Israelites. Tell me, Moses, how did you manage to shake them off?

Moses: When we got to the Reed Sea - that's what we now call the Red Sea - the people were complaining. Then they got scared when they realized the Egyptians were coming after us.

Interviewer: Sorry, Moses, I'm afraid I'll have to stop you there, that's all we have time for today. *(Turns to audience)* So, we leave Moses and the Israelites caught between the Egyptians and the deep

Plagues and Promises

A Life With A Difference

Red Sea. Tune in tomorrow to find out how they survived!

Day 3: Food and Clothes

Interviewer: Hello and welcome to 'A Life with a Difference'. Our featured guest for the whole week is Moses. And you'll remember that yesterday we left him and the Hebrews trapped by Pharaoh's army on the edge of the Red Sea. So, Moses, what happened next?

Moses: I told the people not to worry because God would save us again.

Interviewer: And did he?

Moses: Of course. *(Gesturing with arms)* A column of cloud moved behind us and the Egyptians were in the dark. God told me to lift my staff. I did, and the sea opened up in front of us. We all walked across the dry sea bed.

Interviewer: Incredible! Amazing! *(etc...)*

Aaron: Just as we reached the far shore, the cloud moved and the Egyptians saw us. They followed us.

Moses: More fool them! God told me to stretch out my hand over the waters. I did, and the sea rushed back in over the Egyptian army.

Interviewer: Was that really necessary, since you'd already escaped?

Moses: It was a sign of God's power, a proof that he was the one and only God. Things were different in those days, while God's people were still vulnerable and had no place of their own.

Interviewer: Well, anyway, you were home and dry once you'd defeated the Egyptian army, I suppose?

Aaron: Well, no. We wandered in the Desert of Shur for a very long time and we had problems with fresh water and food and by the time we came to the desert of Sinai, the people were in a real state, complaining, falling out with each other - and us.

Interviewer: I bet you wished you had stayed in Egypt! It seems to me these people were never happy. I guess they had a point, though. How do you feed thousands of hungry people in a place where there are no crops or facilities of any kind? So, Moses, I suppose you were praying for a miracle?

Moses: No. But every time there was a problem, God showed me

You may photocopy this page for use in your Plagues and Promises sessions. © NCEC 1998.

Plagues and Promises

A Life With A Difference

	what to do. There is your miracle.
Interviewer:	*(Taken aback)* Quite! *(Recovering composure)* So what did you do for water in the desert?
Moses:	We found a spring, but they complained the water was too dirty to drink. God spoke to me again, and I threw a piece of wood into the water. The water became sweet and fresh. And there was another instance when they were thirsty and there was no water to be had. God directed my hand again. He pointed out a certain rock, so I hit it with my staff and out gushed water, enough for everyone.
Interviewer:	So, did that stop them complaining then?
Moses:	Only for a while, because any food we had was rapidly running out and there was nothing in that desert which we could pick. Even I was beginning to wonder quite what to do. And, oh dear, did those people moan and complain! Time and time again I was confronted with the question, 'Why have you brought us out of slavery? In Egypt we had meat!'
Interviewer:	But, God to the rescue again?
Moses:	Of course. In fact, food literally rained down from the sky. We called it manna. It was white sticky stuff. You can get a syrupy liquid from the hamada shrubs in the desert, which is similar, but this rained down every morning. I think your audience is being shown something like it at the moment.
	(Pass around bowls of Honey and Banana Whip (page 23) to be tasted)
Interviewer:	So, you miraculously had plenty to eat and drink.
Moses:	Well, yes, but there were rules about the manna given us by God. God often gave us rules about food and drink, because he knows how important they are. We were not to stockpile the manna, but on the day before the Sabbath we were to gather enough for two days. But, as you might imagine, quite a number disobeyed the command – took too much or too little and went to look for it on the Sabbath.
Interviewer:	And when people broke the rules like that, what happened?
Moses:	Well, any extra manna they collected quickly went rotten. And God was angry.
Interviewer:	But you were roaming the desert for years, weren't you?

Resources Section 47

You may photocopy this page for use in your Plagues and Promises sessions. © NCEC 1998.

•••••••••••• **Plagues and Promises** ••••••••••••

A Life With A Difference

	These people had complained about everything so far. I'm sure they weren't happy living on sticky manna and nothing else. Didn't God also provide meat, for variety if nothing else?
Moses:	The quails that migrate, they flew over our encampment at just the right time. So we all had meat in the evenings and bread, of a sort, in the mornings, as God had promised.
Interviewer:	*(To audience)* Right, now, a question. If you had been one of those people in that desert, sometimes hungry, sometimes thirsty, but always moving on: would you rather stay in Egypt under Pharaoh's rule or would you rather stay in the desert, trusting in God to provide for you? Hands up those who would rather have stayed in Egypt. *(Count taken)* And those who would rather be in the desert. *(Count taken) (Ad lib. according to result)*
Interviewer:	Now, I'll admit I'm puzzled here. Why did God set all these rules about something as simple as food and drink? Of course, for special occasions, it appears there were even more rules to remember.
Moses:	You mean the Passover meal, for example?
Interviewer:	Yes. But we have a special guest here today to tell us all about that. Ladies and gentlemen, please welcome Israelite leader Naboth.
	Naboth enters, applause, welcome, etc. (Perhaps he wears a chef's hat?)
Interviewer:	Welcome, Naboth. You've known Moses a long time, yes?
Naboth:	Yes, I knew him in Egypt and I travelled across the desert with him.
Interviewer:	But you're here today to tell us about what happened the day before you left Egypt.
Naboth:	Well, thank you for inviting me onto your programme. And before I tell you about the meal we ate that night, the Passover, I would just like to thank Moses for all he did for our people. Never an easy task, leading so many people, trying to convince them to do things for their own good, and...
	Moses acknowledges this with a smile and a handshake
Interviewer:	But, back to the Passover.

48 Resources Section ••••••••••••••••••••••••••••

You may photocopy this page for use in your Plagues and Promises sessions. © NCEC 1998.

Plagues and Promises

A Life With A Difference

Naboth: Oh. Ah, yes, the Passover. This was a meal Moses told us to prepare. We had lamb and bitter herbs and unleavened bread. We had to paint the lamb's blood on the doorposts and lintel of the houses. We learned afterwards that in all those houses where this had not been carried out, in the houses of the Egyptians, all the first sons died. That was the last plague God sent on the Egyptians, the one that changed Pharaoh's mind. And the Israelite children were safe because we had carried out God's instructions to the letter. Moses had told us exactly what to do.

Interviewer: So this rule about the blood wasn't just a ritual? It was a kind of sign?

Naboth: Yes. The Angel of Death visited Egypt that night, but he passed over the houses marked with lamb's blood.

Interviewer: And were there any other rules for this Passover meal?

Naboth: We had to eat our meal all dressed ready for the journey next day. That was sensible, because it turned out to be the journey of our lives. We took gold and silver with us, and precious things, a lot of it almost thrust at us by the Egyptians because they would give us anything to go away from their land. Pharaoh, too, couldn't be rid of us quickly enough. Was he beginning to realize he had underestimated our God, I wondered. And as I was saying only...

Interviewer: *(Interrupting)* Had he underestimated God, Moses?

Moses: No doubt of it. None of us should underestimate God and what he can do for us.

Interviewer: Thank you, Moses. Thank you, Naboth. I think all those rules make a little more sense now.

Naboth: They're God's way of reminding us about the things that really matter, I think.

Interviewer: Right. Well, join us tomorrow for the next episode of 'A Life With A Difference', when we'll be finding out more about the Hebrews' journey across the desert.

Day 4: Rules and Promises

Interviewer: Hello and welcome to the next instalment of 'A Life with a Difference' in which we have met and are getting to know Moses, the man who led the Israelites into Canaan, the land

Resources Section 49

You may photocopy this page for use in your Plagues and Promises sessions. © NCEC 1998.

Plagues and Promises

A Life With A Difference

he says God promised to them.

One thing I've noticed in this story is that the Israelites were always whining and making demands on poor old Moses. It must have tried his patience, I suppose, even if, as he says, he was less impatient and impetuous than he had been.

Moses is a modest man, so I couldn't tell you while he was on stage, but do you want to know just how many people he was in charge of? There were 600,000 men, never mind all the women and children, all travelling in the desert. Just how does one man keep control of so many? That's what we're here to find out about today - leadership and personnel management, the way God intended it.

So, we turn to our first guest of the evening. I want to introduce you to Moses' father-in-law, Jethro.

Applause as Jethro enters: usual welcoming process.

Interviewer: So, tell us, Jethro, how did Moses cope with all those people?

Jethro: He listened. Not only to me, his father-in-law, but also to the problems and difficulties of vast numbers of people. I felt he was a conscientious judge. He would sit for hours listening to disputes between the people. Usually it was of no real concern to him personally. There's no doubt, Moses set a fine example of unselfish dedication to the public good.

Interviewer: Did you actually travel with Moses, then?

Jethro: No, but we heard what was happening. Eventually, I decided it was time to go to him with Zipporah, his wife, and sons. They had been staying with me as we thought it safer for them all. I know my Zipporah had missed him.

Interviewer: You had a good relationship with Moses, then?

Jethro: Oh, yes, and I was so happy to hear from Moses about the Israelites' adventures and all the miracles that helped them. I had wondered about my son-in-law when he said that God spoke to him through a burning bush, but I believed him now.

Interviewer: But we already know it was not plain sailing for Moses. Didn't you give him some fatherly advice?

Jethro: You see, he was settling disputes from morning till night, wearing himself out. So I told him, 'Delegate some of the responsibility.' There were plenty of able men, ready and will-

You may photocopy this page for use in your Plagues and Promises sessions. © NCEC 1998.

Plagues and Promises

A Life With A Difference

	ing to ease his burden.
Interviewer:	*(To audience)* Do some of us find we take on too much? We feel we can't let people down, sometimes we feel no one else can do it like we do, we're – indispensable, that's the word. Anyone like to comment?
	Open up to discussion; Jethro can join in.
Interviewer:	Thank you all and thank you, Jethro. Anyway, it seems God wanted to help Moses out. We saw yesterday how he gave him rules about meals and food in general. He gave him a set of rules for behaviour, too, to help with disputes. And if modern technology serves us, I think we can see here what those rules were. (*Switch on overhead projector showing an acetate of the Ten Commandments.*) Yes, that's right. Here we see the Ten Commandments.
	Moses received these commands and gave them to the Israelites in a rather dramatic way. But we'll hear all about that from the man himself.
	Moses enters. Usual formalities.
Interviewer:	Let's just set the scene, as you explained it to me earlier. You have reached Mount Sinai, set up camp and on the third day after arrival you go up the mountain to speak to God who instructs you to tell the people he will come in a cloud and from then on the people will believe in you. Am I right?
Moses:	*(Excited, as if reliving the scene)* You are. And God did speak to his people, just as he promised. The mountain erupted and smoked and there was thunder and lightning and a trumpet blast. The people were terrified!
Interviewer:	And they weren't allowed to go near the mountain even if they hadn't been scared. Because it was marked off as sacred, and no one was to go near it except yourself and Aaron?
Moses:	Indeed. I went up the mountain and there God gave to me the Ten Commandments. When I came down the mountain the people were still afraid. Again I went up the mountain, to the very top, where God was.
Interviewer:	I'd like to bring in Aaron, your brother, there because – well, we'll let you, the audience, judge for yourselves.
	Enter Aaron to applause. Usual welcome.

You may photocopy this page for use in your Plagues and Promises sessions. © NCEC 1998.

Plagues and Promises

A Life With A Difference

Interviewer:	Moses was up on the mountain with God, and you were there, in the desert, waiting for him to come back down?
Aaron:	The people were restless, they were worried, when Moses didn't return I think they felt let down, they didn't know what to think. I didn't know what to think! They asked me to make them a god.
Interviewer:	And you did what they asked?
Aaron:	To my shame I did. I told them to bring me all their gold earrings. I melted them down and moulded a golden calf. When it was finished I put up an altar and declared that there was to be a festival to honour this new god.
Interviewer:	So, you and the people gave up on God. Did he give up on you?
Aaron:	No, God never gave up on us, because he had made a promise.
Interviewer:	What promise was that?
Aaron:	He promised Abraham, Isaac and Jacob, our ancient ancestors, that their descendants, these people of Israel, would be 'as numerous as the stars in the sky'.
Interviewer:	So what did he do about your new god, then?
Aaron:	He must have been angry, because he finally sent Moses back to us. He'd been on the mountain for forty days. As you can imagine, when Moses came upon us partying in front of a golden calf, he was angry. That temper of his!
Moses:	*(Interrupting, agitated and angry)* I should say so! I was so angry I threw the tablets of stone on the ground. They broke! God's Commandments in pieces!
Aaron:	Calm down, Moses! It was a long time ago. I'm sorry. I still haven't forgiven myself, really. I was the High Priest, I should have kept faith with God. Maybe then so many of the Israelites wouldn't have died that day.
Interviewer:	And you'd lost the Commandments he gave you as well?
Moses:	Yes, but God told me to take two tablets of stone up the mountain and he wrote down the Commandments all over again. And I showed them to the people a second time.
	(Showing of Commandments again)

Plagues and Promises

A Life With A Difference

Aaron: When he came back his face was shining. It was a wonderful moment.

Moses: God's rules and God's promises to his people. Never to be lost or forgotten again.

Interviewer: Well, that's a sobering thought. *(Pause)* God-given rules for our life. *(Pause)* And these rules helped you stop all those arguments and complaints, Moses? *(Moses nods. Interviewer turns to audience.)* But why did Moses put up with those complaints, those problems? Why did he keep on leading a people who turned away from God even while he was talking to God for them? Tomorrow, we'll be asking Moses some searching questions about why he did what he did. What makes a man like Moses tick? Join us again tomorrow. Until then, goodbye.

Day 5: Dreams and Visions

Interviewer: Hello. Here we are at day number five of 'A Life with a Difference', which has been focusing on the life of Moses. We've heard how Moses led the Israelites across the desert. How God helped him to find food and water for all of them. How Moses passed on all God's rules to them. And how the people were so stubborn that they not only carried on complaining, but even invented a new god as soon as Moses' back was turned. So today, we're going to find out just how Moses kept going against the odds, and how he tried to inspire his people to do the same. And the Ten Commandments we discussed yesterday are at the heart of that.

You'll remember that the rules God gave to Moses were written in fire on stone tablets. They were kept in a box called the Ark of the Covenant, which everyone knows about today courtesy of Indiana Jones. And this Ark was kept in a tent called the Tabernacle. Basically, this was the Israelites' temple.

And here we should recall that, all this time, Moses and the people were where? In the desert. So first, we'd like to ask Moses, how do you go about building a temple in the desert? And, perhaps more to the point, why bother?

Enter Moses to usual welcome.

Interviewer: So now you had to be a builder too.

You may photocopy this page for use in your Plagues and Promises sessions. © NCEC 1998.

Plagues and Promises

A Life With A Difference

Moses: Yes. But I saw myself as building dreams as much as physical buildings. I did it all with God's instructions and help - I could never have done it alone. I've got to admit, even for me, God's plan was like a dream. I could only hope it would come true. The way I see it, God's plans are often hard to understand. Most of us think too much about how and why, when God wants us to dream and aspire. That was why the Israelites had so much trouble understanding God's plan and going along with it.

Interviewer: But you yourself, Moses, you believed it could be achieved?

Moses: Why not? We should all have dreams; it became my ideal, my dream, to reach the promised land of Canaan. And you must remember, I come from a long line of dreamers! There was Joseph, my great, great and many greats more uncle, who interpreted Pharaoh's dreams. Abraham too, another of my ancestors, had dreams that came true.

Interviewer: And there's Jacob, who I had on my show last month. He dreamed of a ladder up to heaven with the angels of God going up and down.

Moses: We have to believe our dreams will come true. And my people certainly thought reaching the promised land was only a dream. The problems we had in the desert were a test of our vision and faith, if nothing else.

Interviewer: And would you say the incident of the burning bush all those years ago acted as an inspiration for you to go forward?

Moses: Without a doubt; and everything else that happened too, you know, the manna, the water, everything really.

Interviewer: But to come back to this Tabernacle, this sacred tent. If you were so concerned about reaching the Promised Land, why stop in the desert to make something like that?

Moses: Because the Commandments and the tent we kept them in were a symbol of God's promise. We needed a visible symbol to remind people that we had hope because God was with us.

Interviewer: But this Tabernacle still had to be built. And I know your right-hand man in this was Samuel, your director of works, along with Bezalel and Oholiab, the craftsmen who made the furniture and ornaments for the Tabernacle.

You may photocopy this page for use in your Plagues and Promises sessions. © NCEC 1998.

Plagues and Promises

A Life With A Difference

Enter Samuel, Bezalel and Oholiab with the usual welcome

Interviewer:	As usual, there were very strict instructions for the building of the Tabernacle, which Moses passed on to you, Samuel? And I understand you are going to try to recreate the building of the Tabernacle for us here today.
Samuel:	Yes, and I've brought with me as many of my men as I could contact after all these years.
Interviewer:	And I think you have a plan, a drawing for us to see, before you start.
Samuel:	Here we are. (*Picks it up from the side of the chair together with pointer and proceeds to explain the plan to audience*) We have a central sanctuary structure and around it a rectangular court, enclosed by curtains. It is 145' long x 70' wide x 7' high or 44m x 21m x 2.1m.(*Demonstrate using the dimensions of the room you are in.*)
Interviewer:	What a building! And Bezalel and Oholiab from the tribes of Judah and Dan, you work in gold and silver?
Bezalel:	Yes, and also precious stones.
Oholiab:	Furniture too.
Interviewer:	Very impressive. But if you were roaming the desert, where did you get all the precious metals and jewels?
Bezalel:	All the materials we needed to build both the Tabernacle and the furniture came from the people. In fact, they gave so much that we had to tell them to stop!
Oholiab:	And, funnily enough, a lot of the precious metals and stones came from the Egyptians, as they gave us all manner of beautiful and precious things just to get us out of their country.
Moses:	I'd like to come in there, if I may. You must also realize that wherever these items came from, the people gave of their best, gave them all willingly, with joy. It was an offering they could make to God. And we all know how good it is to give, especially when we know so much has been given to us. I think finally the people had realized that all I had said was true. They finally accepted that God would help them and so they trusted God in return. As I said earlier, the Tabernacle was to be a symbol for all our hopes and dreams.
Interviewer:	And now we come to the construction of the Tabernacle. So,

You may photocopy this page for use in your Plagues and Promises sessions. © NCEC 1998.

Plagues and Promises

A Life With A Difference

if Samuel is ready, before your very eyes – The Tabernacle.

Enter group of folk to construct the Tabernacle with everyone on stage showing interest and possibly helping.

(Use of smoke machine/dry ice and suitable music)

When all is complete, Oholiab and Bezalel come forward and put the Ark in the centre.

Interviewer: My grateful thanks to each and every one for the parts they have played. Join us next time for the final episode of 'A Life with a Difference'. Goodbye.

Day 6: Praise and Prayer

Interviewer: Good morning and welcome to the last in this current series of 'A Life with a Difference'. And that life belongs to Moses. We have met some of the people who were important in his life – his mother, brother and sister, his wife and father-in-law, some of his people, his craftsmen and finally we shall meet the man who is to succeed Moses as the leader of the tribes of Israel – Joshua.

Enter Joshua. Usual welcome.

Interviewer: You've known Moses a long time. Did you think he was grooming you to take over?

Joshua: At the time, no, I did not, but, looking back, I can see now that he must have had that in mind.

Interviewer: Perhaps you would explain to us.

Joshua: Well it goes back really to when we had a skirmish with a people called the Amalekites. Moses told me to choose the men to fight back. Then I went with him up Mount Sinai the second time. And it was I who mistook the partying and celebrating over the golden calf for fighting!

Interviewer: Go on.

Joshua: Another time, he left me in charge of the Tent of Meeting. I was foolish enough to make a fuss over a couple of men making prophecies, because I thought that was a job just for Moses or Aaron. I was wrong, of course - we all have roles to play, and I understand that now. But Moses wasn't angry about it, he just told me not to be jealous for his sake. And we are very close now. Yes, I'm sure Moses intended all along

You may photocopy this page for use in your Plagues and Promises sessions. © NCEC 1998.

Plagues and Promises

A Life With A Difference

	that I should be his successor and I feel very humble before him, and before God.
Interviewer:	Thank you, Joshua. So before we meet the great man for the last time, and to spare his blushes, I'd like to say a few things about Moses that I feel sure we must all have learned in this series of programmes. The first thing we must have realized about Moses is his amazing success as a leader. The people he led were often unhappy and complaining, and constantly broke the rules he gave them. It's a testament to this man's abilities that he persuaded them to leave Egypt in the first place. We heard how he learned to choose leaders and delegate responsibility. But, most strikingly, Moses led his people in the foundation of their religious beliefs and faith.
	Moses, once a baby in the bulrushes, shy but impetuous and hot-tempered, no orator but powerful. Perhaps we can sum it up with these words:
	'There has never been a prophet in Israel like Moses; the Lord spoke with him face to face.'
	Ladies and gentlemen – Moses.
	Moses enters to great applause, a standing ovation.
Interviewer:	Moses, we're coming to the end of your story. You have a successor, the promised land is in sight. You have led your people and carried out the plan given you by God. Anything to say?
Moses:	*(Obviously quite emotional)* Only a heartfelt thank you to my God and to his people who trusted me enough to see it through. It has all been said. I can hardly speak.
Interviewer:	So Moses reached the promised land of Canaan. He went up from the plains of Moab and the Lord showed him the whole land. At the age of 120, his eyesight was still good and he was as strong as ever.
	Now, let's have a party to celebrate this Life With A Difference!

You may photocopy this page for use in your Plagues and Promises sessions. © NCEC 1998.

Plagues and Promises

A Life With A Difference: The Plague Rap

When Israel was in Egypt's land,
Worked so hard they could not stand.
Beaten and whipped and cursed all day;
By the Nile they would not stay.

God said, 'Let my people go!'
But Pharaoh, he said, 'No!'

The Lord told Moses where to start
To soften hard old Pharaoh's heart.
'Use your staff to show my power,
Egyptians then from you will cower.'

God said, 'Let my people go!'
But Pharaoh, he said, 'No!'

The waters of the Nile turned red;
The fish sank down to the river bed.
No-one there could find a drink,
The water made a dreadful stink.

God said, 'Let my people go!'
But Pharaoh, he said, 'No!'

Then frogs infested all the land,
Everywhere you couldn't stand;
In ovens, beds and cupboards too,
Even splashing in the loo!

God said, 'Let my people go!'
But Pharaoh, he said, 'No!'

Flies then came to buzz around;
Hundreds, thousands on the ground.
The cattle then began to die
Egyptians start to wonder why?

God said, 'Let my people go!'
But Pharaoh, he said, 'No!'

When sores and boils came on their skin
Egyptian strength was wearing thin.
The sky turned black, the thunder roared
And down upon them hailstones poured.

God said, 'Let my people go!'
But Pharaoh, he said, 'No!'

Then greedy locusts came to eat
Anything green beneath their feet.
They ate the fruit, the grass, the grain,
Nothing there will grow again.

God said, 'Let my people go!'
But Pharaoh, he said, 'No!'

Moses raised his hand up high,
An eerie darkness filled the sky.
For three whole days they could not see.
Still Pharaoh said, 'You can't go free.'

God said, 'Let my people go!'
But Pharaoh, he said, 'No!'

God said, 'Now I will get tough!
Pharaoh should have had enough.
All the first-born sons will die
Everyone will shout and cry;
No one will escape the curse.
Things couldn't really get much worse.'

God said, 'Let my people go!'
But Pharaoh, he said, 'No!'

God told his people what to do
When danger it was passing through;
With lamb's blood on their doors outside
The Israelites from death could hide.

God said, 'Let my people go!'
But Pharaoh, he said, 'No!'

Everything went as God had planned,
Pharaoh said, 'No more I'll stand:
Out you go, go on, you're free;
Keeping you's too much for me.'

God said, 'I will lead you now,
And Pharaoh to my name will bow.'

You may photocopy this page for use in your Plagues and Promises sessions. © NCEC 1998.

Plagues and Promises

Resources Section 59

This page may be photocopied for use in your Plagues and Promises sessions. © National Christian Education Council 1998.

Plagues and Promises

My *Plagues and Promises* book

Personal Details

My family name is _____

My first name is _____

Date of birth: _____ Age: _____

Place of birth: _____ Eyes: _____

Shoe size: _____ Height: _____

My favourite job is _____

Other personal details which are important to me:

Fingerprint

Portrait or Photograph

Page 1

The blessing

May the God who made us bless us.

May the God who leads us bless us.

May the God who guards us bless us.

May the God who knows us bless us.

And may we make God's name known always and everywhere. Amen.

60 Resources Section

This page may be photocopied for use in your Plagues and Promises sessions. © National Christian Education Council 1998.

Plagues and Promises

Symbol Stamps

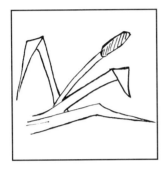

You and Me
Bulrush

Friends and
Enemies
Frog

Food and Clothes
Quail

Rules and Promises
Tablets

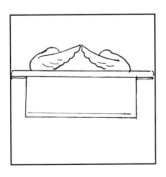

Dreams and Visions
Ark

Praise and Prayer
Rainbow

Resources Section 61

This page may be photocopied for use in your Plagues and Promises sessions. © National Christian Education Council 1998.

Plagues and Promises

WHO'S WHO?
The Twelve Tribes of Israel

Plagues and Promises

The twelve Tribes of Israel claimed their descent from the blessing given by Jacob to his sons, which we can read about in the book of Genesis, chapter 49.

The names are those of Jacob's twelve sons, with the following exceptions:

- Joseph's name is not mentioned. Instead there are two Tribes called after his sons, Ephraim and Manasseh.

- The name of Levi is left out because of his part in a terrible massacre at Shechem. However, in the wilderness the Levites were faithful to God when everyone else was worshipping the golden calf and for this reason the Levites became priests.

Here are the names of the Tribes and the words of Jacob's blessing for each of his sons. Each tribe also had a symbol.

REUBEN

*Reuben, my firstborn, you are my strength and the first child of my manhood,
The proudest and strongest of all my sons.
You are like a raging flood,
But you will not be the most important.*

Plagues and Promises

SIMEON

Simeon and Levi are brothers.
They use their weapons to commit violence.
I will not join in their secret talks,
Nor will I take part in their meetings,
For they killed men in anger
And they crippled bulls for sport.
I will scatter them throughout the land of Israel.
I will disperse them among its people.

JUDAH

Judah, your brothers will praise you.
You hold your enemies by the neck.
Your brothers will bow down before you.
Judah is like a lion,
Killing his victim and returning to his den,
Stretching out and lying down.
No one dares disturb him.
Judah will hold the royal sceptre,
And his descendants will always rule.
Nations will bring him tribute
And bow down in obedience before him.

ZEBULUN

Zebulun will live beside the sea.
His shore will be a haven for ships.
His territory will reach as far as Sidon.

Page 2

---

and his left hand on the head of Manasseh, who was the elder. Joseph was upset when he saw that his father had put his right hand on Ephraim's head; so he took his father's hand to move it to the head of Manasseh. He said to his father, 'Not that way, Father. This is the elder boy; put your right hand on his head.'
His father refused, saying, 'I know, my son, I know. Manasseh's descendants will also become a great people. But his younger brother will be greater than he, and his descendants will become great nations.'
So he blessed them that day, saying, 'The Israelites will use your names when they pronounce blessings. They will say, "May God make you like Ephraim and Manasseh".' In this way Jacob put Ephraim before Manasseh.

EPHRAIM

Ephraim became a very powerful tribe.

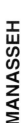

MANASSEH

Manasseh held the largest territory of any of the tribes.

Page 5

Plagues and Promises

ASHER
Asher's land will produce rich food.
He will provide food fit for a king.

NAPHTALI
Naphtali is a deer that runs free,
Who bears lovely fawns.

BENJAMIN
Benjamin is like a vicious wolf.
Morning and evening he kills and devours.
(Benjamin was Jacob's youngest son and the name is often associated with youngest children! The tribe was renowned for the savagery of its exploits.)

Jacob blessed Joseph as he blessed his other sons. However, Joseph's name was not given to a tribe. Instead the Tribes took their names from his two sons, Ephraim and Manasseh.

The story of Ephraim and Manasseh
Joseph brought (his sons) Ephraim and Manasseh to Jacob. Joseph put Ephraim at Jacob's left and Manasseh at his right. But Jacob crossed his hands, and put his right hand on the head of Ephraim, even though he was the younger,

Page 4

ISSACHAR
Issachar is no better than a donkey
That lies stretched out between its saddle-bags.
But he sees that the resting-place is good
And that the land is delightful.
So he bends his back to carry the load
and is forced to work as a slave.

GAD
Gad will be attacked by a band of robbers
But he will turn and pursue them.

DAN
Dan will be a ruler for his people.
They will be like the other tribes of Israel.
Dan will be a snake at the side of the road,
A poisonous snake beside the path,
That strikes at the horse's heel,
So that the rider is thrown off backwards.

Page 3

Resources Section 65

This page may be photocopied for use in your Plagues and Promises sessions. © National Christian Education Council 1998.

Plagues and Promises

Moses Maze

66 Resources Section

This page may be photocopied for use in your Plagues and Promises sessions. © National Christian Education Council 1998.

Plagues and Promises

The Friendship Wordsearch

In this wordsearch are 12 words which are important for making and keeping friendships and good relationships.

When you have marked all the words, the remaining letters, reading from left to right and from top to bottom, spell out something Jesus said about friendship, followed by the Bible reference.

L	S	L	O	V	L	E	Y	O	F	C
O	U	H	R	N	I	E	H	I	O	G
Y	G	H	A	B	S	O	U	M	R	U
A	N	R	A	R	T	S	M	Y	G	R
L	I	O	U	R	E	U	O	S	I	E
T	R	U	S	T	N	E	U	L	V	S
Y	A	F	M	I	I	T	R	A	I	P
R	C	K	C	C	N	H	I	A	N	E
P	T	A	E	R	G	T	W	M	G	C
Y	T	S	E	N	O	H	E	L	E	T
E	V	E	O	P	E	N	N	E	S	S

COMMUNICATE   TRUST   CARING
LISTENING   HONESTY   TIME
LOYALTY   OPENNESS   HUMOUR
FORGIVING   SHARE   RESPECT

This page may be photocopied for use in your Plagues and Promises sessions. © National Christian Education Council 1998.

Plagues and Promises

Templates for Jumping Frog and Egyptian Portrait

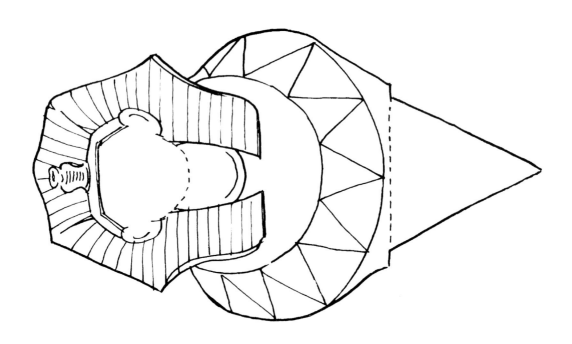

68 Resources Section

This page may be photocopied for use in your Plagues and Promises sessions. © National Christian Education Council 1998.

Plagues and Promises

Festive Feasting

Link each food to the appropriate occasion

• • • • • • • • • • • • **Plagues and Promises** • • • • • • • • • • • •

Grace card template

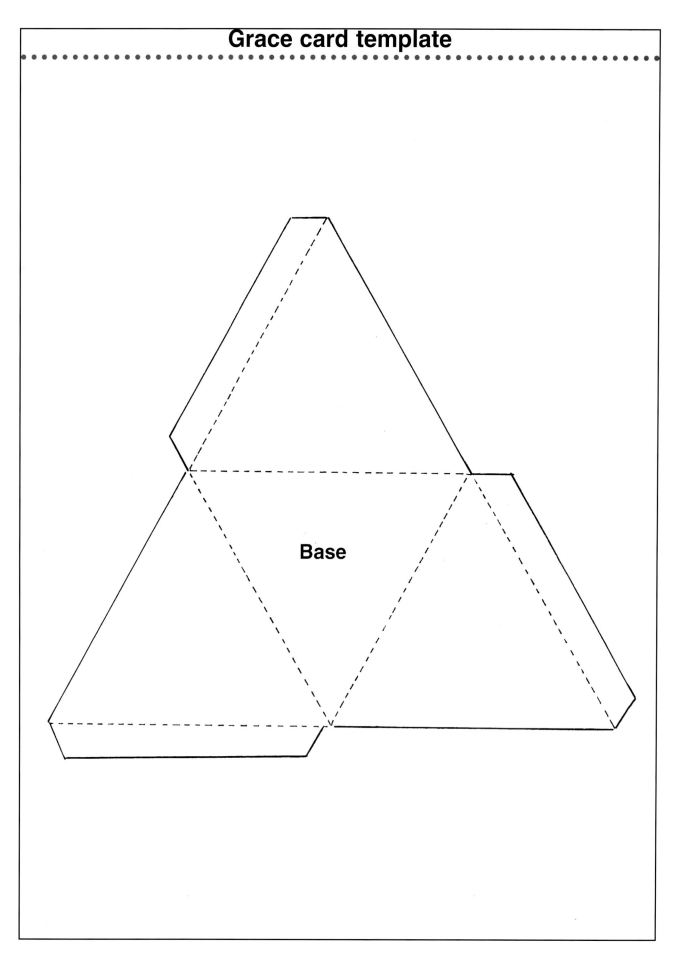

•••••••••••• Plagues and Promises ••••••••••••

How the Jewish people remember their ancestors' escape from slavery in Egypt.

Each year, every Jewish family remembers the way their ancestors escaped from slavery in Egypt. They gather together and prepare a special meal, which they eat at home. The meal begins with a celebration around the dining table and certain particular foods are used. People in the family have special parts to play. The mother lights the candles, the father usually tells the story and the youngest child asks four special questions

The person appointed to take the role of the 'mother' lights the candles and thanks God for the commandments and for the holiday, which has begun at last. Then everyone fills their glasses with 'wine' to celebrate. They praise God in these words:

Be praised, O Lord, King of the Universe, Creator of the fruit of the vine.

The 'father' thanks God for the holiday and then everyone drinks some wine.

After this a bowl of water and a towel are brought to the table. Pass them round so that everyone can wash and dry their hands.

The 'father' now dips the pieces of parsley in the salty water and gives a piece to each person. Everyone holds their piece of parsley and the 'father' explains:

A green vegetable symbolizes the coming of spring and the rebirth of hope. It is dipped into the salty water to remind people of the tears which the Jewish people shed when they were slaves in Egypt. They were able to survive because they dared to hope that one day God would help them to be free.

Then the 'father' takes the middle matzah out from between the other two and breaks it in half. One half is wrapped up in a cloth and someone goes and hides it. The hidden bit has a special name: it is called the Afikomen. The other half is put back between the two whole pieces.

Then the 'father' holds up the plate of matzot and explains:

This is the bread of poverty, which our ancestors ate in Egypt.

He says that he hopes that it can be shared with anyone who is still in need. The plate is put down and covered up again.

The wine glasses are filled up again and then the youngest child asks the four special questions:

Why is this night different from all other nights?
    On all other nights we eat either bread or matzos. Why on this night only matzos?

Plagues and Promises

On all other nights we eat any herbs we wish. Why on this night only bitter herbs?

On all other nights we need not dip any food into any other even once. Why on this night do we have to dip twice?

On all other nights we eat either sitting or reclining. Why on this night do we recline?

Then the 'father' responds:

This night is different from all other nights because on this night we remember the great story of Jewish history, the Exodus from Egypt. Everything we do helps to make the story come alive.

When the Jewish people were slaves in Egypt they had to eat either standing up or sitting on the floor while their masters lay on couches. Because the Passover celebrates their freedom, we eat at Passover reclining as a celebration that we are free.

The Hebrew Bible tells the story of the people of Israel: it tells of the journeys of Abraham, Isaac and Jacob. It tells how Joseph, Jacob's son, became a prince in Egypt and brought his family there to be fed when there was famine. There they stayed for many years. Joseph died and a new king came to the throne in Egypt who knew nothing about Joseph. He was afraid of the Israelites and made them slaves. He even killed their baby boys. But one baby escaped, Moses! God called him to lead his people. Moses asked Pharaoh to set his people free but Pharaoh said no. Then the land of Egypt suffered plagues which were so terrible that Pharaoh changed his mind. Let's remind ourselves what the plagues were:

Everyone names the plagues, one by one, and as they do so, they spill a drop of wine onto their plates.

Blood, frogs, gnats, flies, cattle disease, boils, hail, locusts, darkness, death of the firstborn.

The plagues are a terrible reminder of what happens when people are oppressed. But the Jewish people remember that they escaped and became free and they are very thankful. They use another Hebrew word to thank God. It is Day-ey-nu, which means 'It is enough.' Let's all say it together.

Now we look at the rest of the special foods.

The 'father' takes the lamb bone and says:

The lamb bone is a reminder that on the very first Passover the children of Israel ate a lamb and used its blood to mark their houses so that the Lord 'passed over' them.

Then he takes the matzos and says:

This reminds us of the bread which the people carried out of Egypt. They did not have time

Plagues and Promises

to wait for it to rise.

Then he takes the bitter herb, the horseradish, and says:

This bitter herb reminds us of how bitter life was in Egypt for the slaves, so it is eaten to remind everyone of the bitterness of slavery.

Next everyone praises God and drinks the second glass of wine.

After this everyone washes their hands before the meal. The bowl and towel are brought back and passed around again. The cover is taken off the matzos again and the top and middle pieces are broken up and given to everyone, praising God with the words:

Blessed are You, Lord our God, King of the universe, Who brings forth bread from the earth.

Then everyone eats the matzos.

The 'father' takes some of the horseradish, telling everyone that the bitter herb is a reminder of the bitterness of slavery and the charoset or sweet paste is a reminder of the mortar which the slaves used while building the cities for Pharaoh. The horseradish is dipped into the charoset, a prayer is said and they are eaten.

The last matzah is broken and everyone is given two pieces. They put the bitter herbs and the charoset between them to make a sandwich and eat this.

After this the family eats their festival meal. When it is over, the children in the family all search for the Afikomen that was hidden at the beginning of the service and a reward is given to the person who finds it. It is then broken up and shared out.

After the meal a blessing and more prayers are said, another glass of wine is drunk and the glasses are filled for the fourth time. A big glass on the table is also filled, the cup of Elijah, and people say Psalm 136, a psalm of praise and Psalms 113 - 118. Then people are told that the four cups of wine remind them of God's promise in four different ways:

I will bring you out from under the burdens of the Egyptians.
I will deliver you from their bondage.
I will redeem you with an outstretched arm.
I will take you to be my people.

So the Seder, the special meal, finishes with everyone drinking the fourth cup of wine and praying that next year they will celebrate again in joy, in freedom and in peace.

This page may be photocopied for use in your Plagues and Promises sessions. © National Christian Education Council 1998.

Plagues and Promises

Dress a Priest

Make an Aaron doll

Cutting out will be easier if you can enlarge the drawings on the next page.

Colour the figure, mount it on card and cut it out. Use the diagrams below to make a stand for the figure.

Colour the priest's robes:

Robe (1) - white; colour the embroidery in shades of purple, red, blue and gold.

Tunic (2) - blue; use a gold pen to colour the pomegranates and bells round the hem.

Ephod (3) and *headdress* (4) - decorate with purple, red, blue and gold.

Breastpiece (5) - use a gold or silver pen to colour the background; colour the precious stones as follows:

red	brownish yellow	dark red
green	blue	white
turquoise	white	mauve
pale green	red	mottled brown

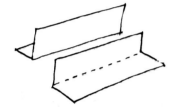
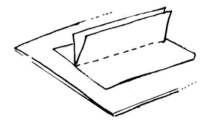
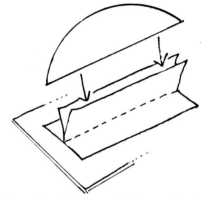

1. Cut 2 thin strips of card and fold as shown.
2. Use a piece of thicker card for a base board.
3. Glue the figure between the two strips of card so that it stands upright.

Dress a person or a doll

Use the pictures opposite as a guide.

Robe - use a long-sleeved, full-length white nightdress.

Tunic - cut a rectangle of blue material, long enough when folded in half to reach from your model's neck to mid-calf and wide enough to meet comfortably at the sides. Cut a slit along the fold for the head opening and cut another slit part of the way down the centre front so that the tunic will go easily over your model's head. Glue some coloured braid around the hem. Use safety pins to secure the sides of the tunic.

Ephod - cut a rectangle of fancy brocade, preferably with some gold on it. Follow the same procedure as for the tunic.

Breastpiece - cut a square of the same brocade and attach long golden ribbons to the corners to tie it on. Glue four rows of coloured sweet wrappers onto the front to represent the precious stones, following the pattern above as far as possible.

Headdress - cut a headband out of card to fit your model's head. Staple a large circle of white material to the card. Stuff with scraps of material or tissue paper to give the headdress some shape. Glue some blue ribbon over the card to hide the staples.

Plagues and Promises

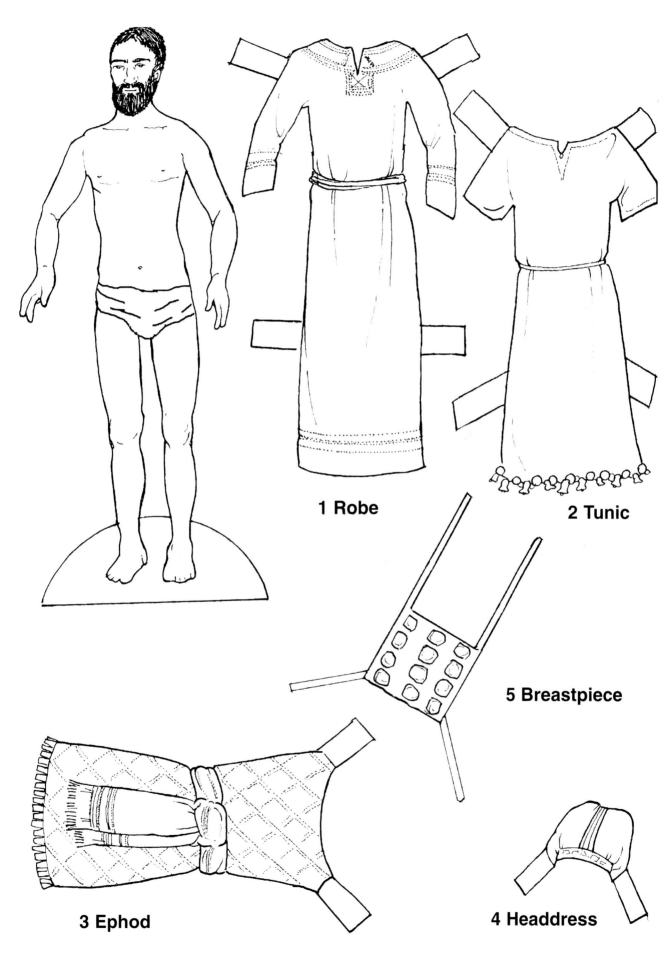

1 Robe

2 Tunic

5 Breastpiece

3 Ephod

4 Headdress

Resources Section 75

This page may be photocopied for use in your Plagues and Promises sessions. © National Christian Education Council 1998.

Plagues and Promises

Spot the Differences

76 Resources Section

This page may be photocopied for use in your Plagues and Promises sessions. © National Christian Education Council 1998.

Plagues and Promises

The Ten Commandments

1. I am the Lord. I am the one who gave you your freedom. No other god is worth worshipping.

2. Don't worship models, carved images and idols. Never reduce me to the size of a doll, and don't try to guess what I look like.

3. Be careful how you use my name. It's not a swear word, and it's not to be taken lightly.

4. Keep one day a week as my special day. Enjoy a rest, and make sure everyone else does too.

5. Look up to your father and mother. Families belong together, and must love each other. A happy nation can only be built out of happy families.

6. Always respect the life of others.

7. Always respect marriage, and be loyal to your own partner.

8. Don't steal.

9. Don't tell lies.

10. Don't be jealous of other people. Envy leads on to stealing and murder, so stop it before it starts! God has made you to be yourself, not to spend your time wishing you were someone else.

From the Fount Children's Bible *by Andrew Knowles, reprinted by permission of HarperCollins Religious*

This page may be photocopied for use in your Plagues and Promises sessions. © National Christian Education Council 1998.

Plagues and Promises

I have a dream...

78 Resources Section

This page may be photocopied for use in your Plagues and Promises sessions. © National Christian Education Council 1998.

Plagues and Promises

Cherubim Template

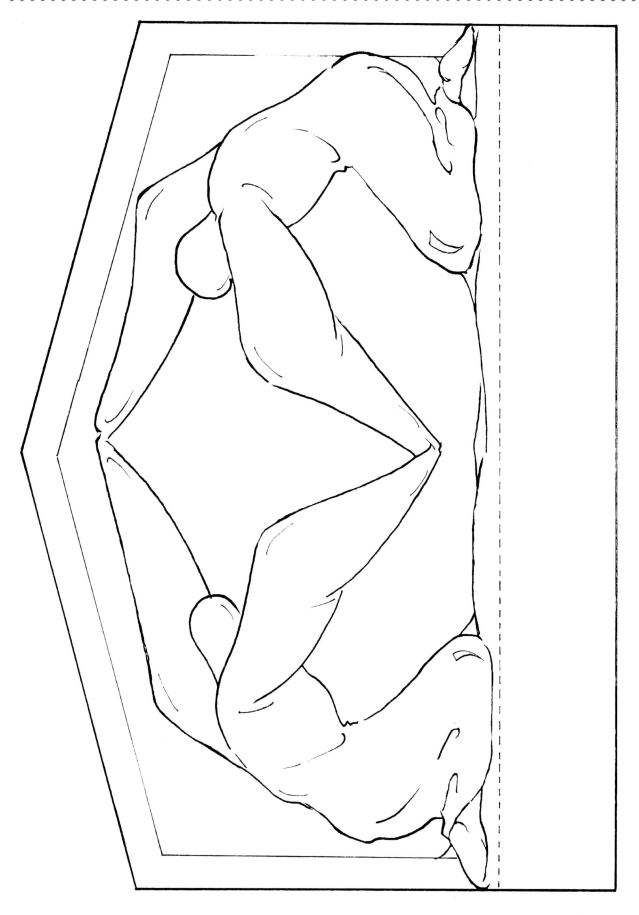

Resources Section 79

Plagues and Promises

Chooser Template

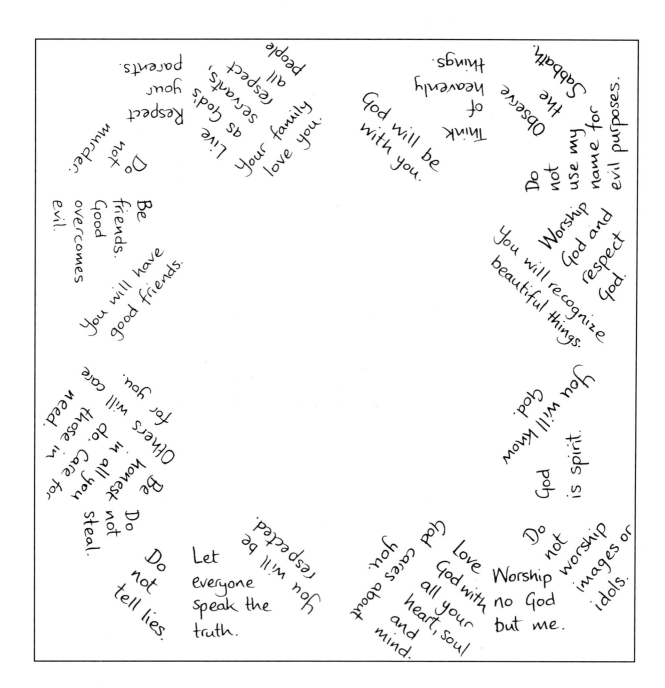

80 Resources Section

This page may be photocopied for use in your Plagues and Promises sessions. © National Christian Education Council 1998.